Working for Glory

A Theology For

Doing Work that Really Matters

By Keith M. Welton

EVERTRUTH

Damascus, MD

Tony,
 So grateful for your
love of reading + writing!
It has sharpened me
in many ways
 K

Published by EverTruth
26700 Ridge Rd Damascus, MD 20872

Cover design by Martin D. Stanley
Cover photo credits:
© Pablo Scapinachis | Dreamstime.com—Grunge Industrial Background
© Eszawa | Dreamstime.com—Old Antique Frame
© Daburke | Dreamstime.com—Time Money Management Watch Silver Dollars
Savings

ISBN Paperback 978-0-9914030-1-1
eBook ISBN 978-0-9914030-2-8

Dedicated to Amanda,
my greatest helper, best critic, strongest encourager,
unwavering friend, and most joyful companion,
without whom this book would not be.
"Many women do noble things,
but you surpass them all" (Prov 31:29).
And as I like to say, "You are the jam in my jelly roll."
I love you with all my heart!

Contents

Introduction

When you drive in to work does it feel like you are going in to do something great and glorious? Most of us would say no. Let's face it, work is hard, and there are things we don't like about it. We are confronted with monotonous repetition, hard tasks, difficult situations, quirky coworkers, and unpleasant customers. There are certainly other things we all could (and probably would like) to be doing, and work interrupts these. We also get worn down, because we sacrifice to work all day every day and hear very little appreciation for what we do. Work doesn't seem so great, and the unpleasant parts often color our attitude of work as a whole. We then work solely for income or vacations only to discover how fleeting and unsatisfying they are. When this happen, we walk into the office discouraged, questioning if what we do on the job matters at all.

The Bible speaks to this disillusionment and lights a path for us to see that work really does matter. God created us for his glory (Isaiah 43:7), and work is a major opportunity to glorify him. This revelation brings meaning, purpose, and significance to all we do in life. It puts things in their proper framework. It also brings great responsibility. We are not to work for our glory but for God's glory, and that means how we work is important too. I have entitled this book *Working for Glory* to remind us of both the privilege and responsibility in work. It's to remind of a higher calling in all that we do, and the purpose for writing the book is to help us understand *how* to glorify God through work. I want every person engaging each day, not regretful for where they are or apologetic for what they are doing, but full of faith they have an opportunity to live for the purpose they were created. I want them focused on that goal!

Now knowing that we are "working for God's glory" is helpful in pointing us to a larger main goal, but there is a danger of this goal being too broad. If something is left too broad it can mean almost anything, and when something means anything it means virtually nothing. Some people say they are working for God's glory one moment and the next they are ripping off customers. Others say it to justify preaching to their coworkers all day and not getting any of their work done. Some use it to explain why they won't fire an employee whose poor work is destroying the company. Some say it but have no clue how or if their work really connects to advancing God's kingdom. Glorifying God in the workplace is clearly something we should want to do, but most Christians in the workplace will readily admit they need a little more definition and nuance on how to do it. Having seen so many people struggle with questions like these is what led me to write this book, and I hope it will help you understand more clearly how your work can truly be done to the glory of God.

Why a Theology for Work?

Now, you may be saying to yourself, "Why a theology of work? Couldn't I get the same thing from a 20 second perusal of 'Chicken Soup for the Soul?' This theology stuff for work seems a bit out of place." After all people who read theologies want elaborate explanations for things like God's sovereignty and human responsibility, but people concerned or interested in business and work just want to know how to get things done; they don't need theology! I actually had a prominent Christian business leader tell me he wasn't interested in any kind of theology at all, and I think his sentiments represent many other Christians in the workplace.

I have spent time in both the theological and business worlds, so I am acutely aware of how different these spheres are from each other, but I am equally aware how they can and should join together. Before you discard this book thinking it's of no use for either business people or theologians, let me tell you why I think it is exactly what people in the workplace need. Right thinking always precedes right living. If you are going to work effectively to the glory of God you need to think rightly about what you are doing. Failure to think rightly will lead to practical failure. The amount of weight placed on us and the powerful pull of the world experienced at work demands substantive answers for why we do or don't' do certain things. Relying on the "Chicken Soup for the Soul" reading right before you head out the door won't give the support needed for when you have to cut a department or show up for yet another day at a dead end job. Such answers are like using tooth picks to hold up a bridge. They will not support the weight we encounter each day at the office, nor do they help us understand the complex issues we face. We need solid answers that give real support and direction to the many different situations and circumstances we find ourselves in while on the job.

Having a right understanding of God is essential for us to answer questions about work. Simply put theology is the study of God: knowing who God is, what he demands from us, and how he has created the world to function rightly should be the foundation of all we think, do, and feel. Our theology will guide our practice. Indeed whether we realize it or not we all have a theology that is undergirding our lives. It has been said "what we think about God is the most important thing about us."[1] If we think God is disinterested in work then we too will be disinterested and may never pursue it with the intensity he desires. If we think he is indifferent to *how* we work then we may be tempted to commit all kinds of atrocities in the workplace. What we think about God— our theology—is pivotal to understanding how we should live and work in the world. Getting this right is the first step in making sure we are working for what matters.

Now that we have seen how important it is to have a theology for work, let me tell you another goal I have. It is to give you a theology of work that is practical, that is not abstract or merely cognitive, but that connects to everyday life. We need a deep theology that holds up to the weights and complexities faced every day in the office. Good theology always has practical effects. I hope this book will help you both to think rightly and work effectively—all to the glory of God.

Lastly, I also hope this book will help you understand other parts of life besides work. Work touches on important things such as our purpose in life, what we are created for, and why we face so many difficulties. In order to work effectively in the world we need to understand how God ordered the world to function and where things like hard work, discipline, and even rest fit in. We also need to understand the vital place of God's word and the church, and

---

[1] A.W. Tozer, *Knowledge of the Holy* (San Francisco: Harper Collins, 1961), 1.

how they relate to and aid us in life and work. All of these are basic elements of life, and yet our present culture is largely confused and confounded by them. If we are going to work for God's glory it is essential to have a right understanding (right theology) of life and how God designed the world to function. These are important topics for us today, and I hope this books helps you better understand these basic parts of life.

An Overview

Let me now give you a brief outline, so you know what lies ahead and how it fits together. As with any book, this book makes the most sense if you read the chapters in order, but each chapter is written to stand on its own, so you can read what is pressing or what interests you. It won't hurt my feelings if you pragmatist choose to skip around. The book is structured in three main parts with Part I focused on showing God's purpose for work and how it is done to his glory. Part II looks at major obstacles that prevent or hinder us from doing work to God's glory. Part III focuses on how wisdom and rest play a part in working rightly and effectively in the world.

Part I. Glorifying God in Work: Chapter 1: This chapter lays a biblical foundation for work that helps us withstand the tide of unbiblical notions of work swirling around us today. It shows the place and purpose God has for work and also the ways God gifts and equips people to do work. Chapter 2: This chapter looks at the chief goal of life and work—the glory of God. It examines some common ways we fail to glorify God in work, and it also explains how work can rightly lead to this chief goal. Chapter 3: This chapter discusses the relation of ministry to work. It gives an understanding for the place of common grace—that is doing our jobs well, serving others, and seeing the difference it can make in the world. It also deals with the place of God's word, the church, and godly ambition. Chapter 4: This chapter deals with the ethics of work and builds upon our calling to work in God's image. Our work should reflect the God we serve, so the characteristics that describe God should also be present in our work.

Part II. Challenges in Work: Chapter 5: This chapter discusses the implications of the curse on work. We need to understand the roots of the difficulties that confront in the workplace and learn how to think about them biblically. Chapter 6: Because work is done under the curse, there will be disappointments—that is seasons of prolonged difficulty. This chapter explains how to prepare for such seasons and also how to persevere through them when they inevitably come. Chapter 7: It is just as common to worship work as it is too think little of it. This chapter deals with the prevalent temptation to idolize work, and it gives sobering reason for resisting this tendency.

Part III. Working Effectively and Rightly in the World: Chapter 8: If we are going to glorify God in work it will mean getting work done. This chapter examines some of the essential biblical components of what it takes to get things done in the world such as diligence, prudence, shrewdness, and many others. Chapter 9: Any book on work would not be complete without a treatment of rest. Working effectively requires resting effectively. This chapter explains God's true intent for rest and gives some practical tips for how we can rightly observe it.

As you read this book, please take the time to look at the verses referenced in each section. Write them down. Put them on your computer monitor. Memorize them. Let Scripture be what ultimately guides you. My hope is that this book would simply be a tool God uses to help you understand his word better. And lastly, think often of Christ. When you feel convicted of things you've done wrong remember he died for your sins, when you see things you think you will never get right remember it was only Christ who lived a sinless life, when you make new commitments regarding the way you work look to him for strength. Above all think often of Jesus' work of redemption and remember it is only Christ and what he has done for us that gives meaning and significance to all that we do. All our work and effort is simply an offering of thanks to him.

Chapter 1

The Foundation of Work—A Privileged Calling

"And God said to them, "Be fruitful and multiply and
fill the earth and subdue it and have dominion
over the fish of the sea and over the birds of the heavens
and over every living thing that moves on the earth."
Genesis 1:28 (ESV)

The foundation of a house is seldom noticed, but its importance is felt in every square inch. This concrete mass is the mainstay that gives stability and support to the entire house. If the ground beneath it sinks or a tree root works its way in, a foundation can be weakened and the structural integrity compromised. Such a disruption sends compounding effects shimmering up the walls. The framing of the house falls out of alignment and weak spots form. Doors and windows will not close. Floors sag and slope. Walls will bow. Chimneys and porches may separate from the house, and creaks go moaning through the hallways. A house that once seemed so strong and impenetrable is left unstable and vulnerable to the threats of storms and winds.

A foundation is the core component providing support for other elements to be built on, and both the concept and importance of strong foundations carry over to many other disciplines, principles, and even beliefs. So how is your foundation for *work*? Is it stable or is it failing? There is no hiding the fact that many people are apathetic toward work today, and this seems to reveal a fault in the foundation. Many people think work is a curse. Others think it is a necessary evil that must be done to enjoy other parts of life. Few people value work and even fewer are excited about it, and if we are not careful this attitude can destroy any joy or purpose we might have.

On any given day we all experience threats that attempt to undermine our work. While driving to work, we hear songs, DJs,

1

and bumper stickers broadcast there are better things to be doing than working. At the office, much of the day's conversation is spent hearing people talk about how hard their work is, and even hearing peers (people in our position) talk about how disappointing their job (our job) is. We watch some people work mechanically with little enthusiasm and others dodge work like it's the plague. After a long hard day at the office, we finally come home only to hear our parents chatter ceaselessly about their latest vacation and how great retirement is. Apathy toward work is everywhere, and it confronts us on everything from why we have to work to why we have the jobs we have.

Like a menacing tree root, this apathy can creep in and disturb the foundation of even the most dedicated workers. When this happens, suddenly we are showing up to work with weak backbones, waning ambition, sagging faces, and moaning voices—wondering if what we do every day matters at all.

If we are going to withstand the bombardment of apathy threatening us on the job, we need a stable foundation. Fortunately, God has given us his word and building our lives on it is like building our foundation on a solid rock that will not fail (Luke 6:47-48). For this reason, we turn now to examine his word and build a biblical foundational of work that provides solid answers on everything from why we work to why we have the jobs we have.

1.1 Work is a Fundamental Privilege of Life

Many people question why they have to work. I certainly did in my youth. I sought to avoid work altogether. I valued having fun and did as little as possible to get by. I took jobs that were easy and required the least effort. Doing a book report for school meant going to the computer to print off one of my older sister's from a previous year. In high school, a friend and I even turned in his fifth-grade sister's science fair project for our Senior Science Project. I never saw that project, but somehow we passed and even won an award (must have been a smart fifth grader). While I got away with some things, there were many others I didn't. I was struggling to make it in life and constantly disappointed. No matter how hard I tried to avoid working it always caught up with me.

After becoming a Christian in college, I started reading the Bible for the first time, and that was when I first saw the important place of work. Frankly, I was shocked to find work appear in the first chapter of Genesis and stand as God's first command to people. As we develop a new understanding of work, it is only appropriate to start here in the beginning of the Bible. Genesis 1:26 and 28 read,

> Then God said, "Let us make man in our image, after our likeness. And let them have dominion over the fish of the sea and over the birds of the heavens and over the livestock and over all the earth and over every creeping thing that creeps on the earth" .... And God blessed them. And God said to them, "Be fruitful and multiply and fill the earth and subdue it and have dominion over the fish of the sea and over the birds of the heavens and over every living thing that moves on the earth." (ESV)

The command to work came before the first sin, in fact it came before people had done anything at all. It came as God's original plan and stands as a central part of what people were created to do in the world. As Leland Ryken said, "The very fact that God commanded such work shows that human work is part of the divine plan for history."[1] Work is not an accident or result of the fall but rather an intentional design for people. God created people to do something—to extend dominion, and work is a central part of that.

Genesis 1:28 also highlights the importance of work as it is one of two basic commands given to people. The first command is to "be fruitful and increase in number," which is essentially to marry and have children. The second is to have dominion. Theologians have often labeled these two commands the cultural mandate, because they permeate every culture, nation, tribe, tongue, and land. Every nation and people needs to engage in these

---

[1] Leland Ryken, *Redeeming the Time* (Grand Rapids: Baker Books, 1995), 174.

3

two practices in order to survive. Work is a basic and necessary component of life. It is the means by which every person eats (2 Thess 3:10). No one is exempt from it, therefore we should not think it an optional part of life.

Work is a major component of human life, and so it only makes sense that it forms a major component of how our time should be spent. Following the pattern of creation, Exodus 20:9 says, "Six days you shall labor and do all your work." It is work and not vacation that is to be tended to the majority of time. In the words of Martin Luther, "Man was created not for leisure but for work."[2] People were created to work and be productive, not sit around all day playing video games, watching movies, or vacationing. We are to work and be fruitful, and those who find themselves working the majority of their days have not erred but rather are following God's intended pattern for human life.

We are commanded to work, but there is a deeper more basic sense in which work forms a part of our purpose in the world. It is a part of who we are and what we were created to do. "Work is a fundamental dimension of man's existence on earth,"[3] and to not work is to lose a dimension of what it means to be human. When we refuse to work, we refuse part of God's purpose and plan for our lives. Any time something goes against the purpose for which it was created, problems and frustration appear. It's like riding a bike through the sand or driving a car in water. When we go against God's purpose and try to define life without work, we experience problems and frustration. This is where I was at before I knew Christ. Grasping God's intention helped me throw off wrong expectations and discover what I was created to do. As I embraced this dimension of existence, life started to make sense and also became more enjoyable. Living according to my purpose brought a newfound satisfaction and delight.

Some people may find it only mildly encouraging to discover work is a basic command and fundamental dimension of life. To them it's like someone saying, "You're created to work so

---

[2] Martin Luther, *Luther's Works: Lectures on Genesis 1-5*, vol 1 (Saint Louise: Concordia Publishing House, 1958), Expositions of Genesis 2:14.

[3] John Paul II, *Encyclical On Human Work: Laborem Exercens* (Boston: Daughters of St Paul, 1981), 11.

just do it!" It's not very inspiring. This is where understanding the privilege of work helps greatly. God's purpose comes through loud and clear in the word "dominion" used in Genesis 1:26. Dominion means to rule over something and indicates the possession of authority over another to direct, lead, or govern them. Dominion is in fact a privileged opportunity given to us by God to rule over and govern his creation.

The word "dominion" may bring to mind the territory over which a king, president, or other imperial leader reigns, and that is exactly what should be thought of. The call to exercise dominion reflects royal language,[4] and by being granted dominion, people are entrusted with a royal calling to reign over a part of the world. Just as we would be honored to receive the throne of a king and gladly reign over a nation from a palace, so also dominion should be seen as a great privilege to reign as a king over a particular area. As we work over computers, fields, spreadsheets, or other people, we should not view it as slavery, but as a great privilege to lead and direct a portion of God's creation. Through work we are able to reign over creation even if our throne is a chair in a cubicle.

Now, some of us may have trouble reconciling this privileged view of work with the difficulties we encounter every day in the office. However, Genesis 1 does not give us a romanticized view of work detached from reality. In verse 28, dominion is connected with subduing. To "subdue" implies that the thing being subdued is resistant to the one subduing; therefore some sort of coercion is required if the subduing is to take place.[5] Effort, force, strategy, and perseverance are required to work effectively. Work is a fundamental privilege, but it was never intended to be easy. Just as a great king does not stand over a peaceful and prosperous kingdom without much effort, so also reigning over our respective kingdoms with peace and prosperity will require much effort, but the difficulty should never take away from the privilege that it is.

---

[4] Victor Hamilton, *The Book of Genesis* (Grand Rapids: William B. Eerdmans Publishing Company, 1990), 138.
[5] R. Laird Harris, Gleason Archer, and Bruce Waltke, *Theological Wordbook of the Old Testament*, (Chicago: Moody Press, 1980), 430.

My incorrect view of work as an optional and unimportant part of life showed my lack of understanding, but even more importantly, it caused me to miss one of the most foundational and important privileges God gave to people. My contempt toward work had actually robbed me of purpose and pleasure. I was provoked to find I was created to work and roused to see the privilege, but still unsure what I was supposed to work toward.

1.2 Furthering God's Creative Purposes

As we seek to grow in our understanding of work, one of the greatest lessons comes not from a command but an example. Typically when a person starts a new job, one of the first things the boss has that person do is shadow a veteran for a few days to learn the ropes. The message sent is loud and clear. See what that person does, and do it like they do. The picture of work done properly is worth a thousand words. Likewise, one of the most compelling pictures of work comes in God's example. Genesis 2:2 says, "And on the seventh day God finished his work that he had done, and he rested on the seventh day from all his work that he had done" (ESV). This verse speaks of the last day of creation and shows that on this day God rested from work. God is a God who works, and we are to follow his example of work.

The author of dominion and work rests, and in doing so reminds everyone he has been working. God himself has been extending dominion over the earth. The earth was formless, empty, and dark (Gen 1:2), but now has shape (land, sea, sky), is teaming with life (fish, birds and animals), and has lights decorating and governing the day and night (1:3, 14). God has taken an inhospitable world and formed it to be a place in which life can flourish. His work is good and provides order and life to the world.

God's example of work gives direction and purpose for our work. The implication of God's work, man created in the image of God, and the cultural mandate is that people should continue the work that God has begun. As Leland Ryken has said, work is to "carry on God's delegated task for his creatures, making the fullness of creation fuller."[6] Work is part of God's plan for developing the entire world and furthering his dominion. As his image bearers, all people are to have a role in furthering God's reign by exercising dominion over creation. The task of cultivating the world to be a place that is good and full of life, vibrancy, and order is achieved by people continuing God's work through their dominion. God's example to better the earth and bless others through work is a guiding illustration for our work.

By giving people the gift of dominion, God invites us to be co-creators with him and participate in the shaping of the world.[7] God is essentially entrusting to humanity the distinct privilege of filling the earth by cultivating part of his creation. Whatever the means by which we work, we are reining over that area as God's chosen representative and should seek to further his creative purposes. It may be a government official trying to establish peace in an area of violence, a contractor building houses that enhance life, or a teacher equipping children to succeed in the world. All these are opportunities to rule over other things or people in order to better the world. They are extending God's creative purposes by spreading goodness and order throughout the world.

When we see that our work is a means of following God's example it transforms our approach to work. We begin to enjoy work as an opportunity to bring good to others and the world. Going to the office each day is no longer about having to work or working for the weekend, but it is about furthering God's life-enhancing purposes.

This truth can change our perspective on work in dramatic ways. When our purpose in work begins to be more like God's purpose, our attitude will also begin to reflect God's attitude. God's work in creation does not look at all like toil but, in the words of Ryken, "more like the exuberance of an artist. It is joyous, self-expressive, and energetic."[8] Work is a means through which human creativity can express itself, and just as Genesis 1

---

[6] Ryken, 175.

[7] R. Paul Stevens. *The Other Six Days* (Grand Rapids: William B. Eerdmans Publishing Company, 1999), 98. See also 1 Cor 3:9 where synergoi means coworkers.

[8] Ryken, 160.

presents God as the exuberant author full of dignity, creative expression, and majestic responsibility, so also this should characterize our dominion. Whether it is an artist decorating offices to create the appropriate ambience for rooms or an engineer designing the structural supports to stabilize that office—both demonstrate exuberant creativity to bring goodness and order to the world. Such exuberance and creativity are the overflow of having a God-ward orientation toward furthering God's creative intentions.

Seeing work as an opportunity to further God's purposes also helps us see the importance of being committed to work. Work is an important means of influencing the world, and it is a tragedy that most people today reject it as a meaningful part of their lives. People win the lottery and quickly decide not to work anymore. Many college students sit around doing nothing, content to live off their parents. For others, the startup business finally takes off and they begin thinking they don't need to show up to the office. It's sad that when people acquire significant power or money, most decide not to work. Such an attitude denies the value of work as a great means of doing good to others and bringing order to the world. It is ironic that the supreme being of the universe does something that most people would not think to do if they were in his position—work. God does not need to work and has no obligation to work, which is very much unlike us who both need to it for sustenance and are commanded to do it, and yet he works. God is a God who works (Gen 2:2, Mark 6:3), and his example of bringing goodness to the world should provoke us.

The work God does should inform our purpose, and this alters our attitude and commitment. God resolutely works to bless others and bring goodness to the world, and we have the wonderful privilege of sharing in that process with him. The purpose of work is much more profound than what we typically think. Work is important, and by following God's example we too can do work that really matters. Through work we have the glorious privilege of furthering God's purposes in the world.

1.3 The Dignity and Responsibility of Work

One reason people often become disillusioned with work is because all too often we see it done incorrectly. We work with a harsh boss or get ripped off by someone who doesn't care about people or God's purposes, and we begin to dread going to work. There are countless instances of work gone bad that will cause us to dislike work and be skeptical of talking positively about dominion. Such examples shouldn't lead us to reject work, but rather it demonstrates the need to do work rightly. The dignity of work should always point to the responsibility of work.

One of my wife's favorite movies is about a young, brash and irresponsible prince who is challenged by a young lady for his inability to appreciate and take seriously his royal position. At a pivotal moment in the movie, the prince callously overlooks a great injustice done to a beggar, and the princess sternly rebukes him for not using his position to provide justice and says to him, "With great privilege comes great responsibility." What the prince needed to realize is exactly what we all need to realize.

Work has great dignity, because it is a unique opportunity to image the living God. Our work is to represent God and care for a portion of his creation. What we do in work affects those under us, around us, and even over us. Caring for the things of God as we do is no light matter. It is an opportunity to stand over creation as an instrument of good. It is full of dignity, and we should look on our work and stand in awe that God entrusted us to care for a part of his creation (Psalm 8). At times work may seem unimportant, but as the things we rule over were made by God and belong to him, our work is always significant, and we must prove faithful with it.

We have a responsibility to work rightly, so it cannot be done carelessly or in just any manner. The way we work is to be informed by Genesis 1:26, which states that God created people in his image. People are called to rule as God rules, and this brings immediate responsibility and clear ethical standards. We are, as Bruce Waltke says, "to be distinguished by our Godlike compassion in connection with our ruling. Like God we are to be merciful kings."[9] God does not reign as an overbearing and greedy tyrant, but as a compassionate and caring lord. He commands work yet provides a day off; he commands obedience yet sends his Son to die for sinners. His example of dominion should inform how we work. We are created in his image and "what is expected of man is responsible care over that which he rules."[10]

Dominion can be dangerous to talk about, because people are a fallen image, and sin can lead some to abuse their calling. This is why many passages that talk about dominion talk about not ruling "ruthlessly" or "harshly" (Lev 25:43, 46, 53, Isaiah 14:6, Ezek 34:4). Too often we neglect responsible care of others in order to benefit ourselves. We work for our own gain and not the good of others: bosses are harsh and demeaning to their employees, CEO's lie to investors about the financial status of their firms, and companies ruthlessly treat employees like low-grade commodities. In doing so, they fail to responsibly demonstrate the God-like influence their glorious privilege demands.

Our responsibility in work is to care for God's creation by ruling as God rules and extending his purposes through the world. To do this rightly, we must make much of God in work and esteem him above all other things. We have a glorious privilege in work, but we must remember work is not for our own glory. It is to be done for the glory of God. 1 Corinthians 10:31 says, "whatever you do, do it all to the glory of God." This is what sets us on the right course for doing work that really matters, and that means we should all be working for glory—his glory.

Work can be done in a good or bad manner, with a redemptive or destructive effect, either for the glory of God or for his defaming. All work matters, and it matters how we do it. If we are to succeed in work it will be by putting God first and honoring him in all we do. The glory of God is the hinge that connects both the significance and responsibly of all work.

---

[9] Bruce Waltke, *Genesis* (Grand Rapids: Zondervan, 2001), 71.
[10] Hamilton, 138.

1.4 All Work that Honors God is Good Work

Many people hear about the privilege and significance of glorifying God in work, but inevitably think it just doesn't apply to certain fields—in other words they think some work is insignificant or worthless. I have spent most of my adult life working in ministry, and I even spent a few years teaching Greek to men training for pastoral ministry. Telling people you teach Greek causes many reactions; the most common is a perplexed stare that seems to reveal them questioning the usefulness and legitimacy of your job. As I would see each blank stare and furrowed brow, I too would question the significance of my job. If we fail to grasp the variety of ways God has given us to glorify him through work, we will either question the legitimacy of our work or the work of others.

In the Middle Ages, people esteemed the work of ministry and thought it more pleasing to God than all other work. This was a misguided notion that many teachers faithful to the scriptures challenged. One of them was William Tyndall, who said, "While the washing of dishes and preaching the word of God represent different human activities, as 'touching to please God,' there is no difference."[11] Tyndale rightly understood there are many ways to glorify God, and we should not denigrate anything that glorifies him.

God has given us many diverse ways to have dominion. When God said to rule over the fish of the sea and the birds of the air, over the livestock, over all the creatures that move along the ground, and over all the earth (Gen 1:26), he gave the ability to rule over many things in many diverse ways. This sets the stage for seeing the many different forms of dominion mentioned in the Bible, which include ambassador (2 Cor 5:20), armor bearer (Judges 9:54), athlete (2 Tim 2:5), baker (Gen 40:1), banker (Matt 25:27), blacksmith (1 Sam 13:19), builder (2 Kings 12:11), carpenter (Mark 6:3), doorkeeper (2 Kings 22:4), emperor (Acts 25:25), farmer (2 Tim 2:6), goldsmith (Isaiah 40:19), guard (1 Sam 22:17), jailer (acts 16:23), innkeeper (Luke 10:35), king (Gen

---

[11] Alister McGrath, *Reformation Thought* (Oxford: Blackwell Publishing, 1999), 256.

14:1), lawyer (Acts 24:1), mason (2 Kings 12:12), midwife (Gen 35:17), moneylender (Exodus 22:25), musician (Psalm 68:25), pharaoh (Gen 41:55), philosopher (Acts 17:18), physician (Jer 8:22), priest (Gen 14:18), poet (Acts 17:28), queen (1 Kings 10:1), shepherd (1 Sam 21:7), soldier (John 19:23), tax collector (Matt 10:3), tentmaker (Acts 18:3), silversmith (Judges 17:4), teacher (1 Chron 25:8), weaver (Exodus 35:35), woodsman (2 Chron 2:10), writer (Psalm 45:1), and countless others.

What is said in Genesis about dominion is as important as what is not said. There could have been a more specific phrase for work, like a word that applied to the agricultural fields, or maybe one with a military connotation, or maybe one that referred to white collar positions. Instead the term is broad and allows for innumerable types of work and dominion to be done by people with various gifts, abilities, backgrounds, and even limitations, and all these forms of work are clothed with dignity and significance.

It may be surprising to see some roles on a list of approved jobs in scripture, such as a pharaoh, but it is clear in scripture that what is more important than a job title is if the person in the job positively images God or not. Titles are not condemned, but the actions of people are. Kings are rebuked not because the position of a king is wrong, but because the kings did not glorify God (1 Kings 15:26). Any position can be distorted and manipulated, and this is why it is important to honor God by ruling as he rules. For example, some may think it wrong to be a tax collector, because in biblical times they were detested for collecting more than they should, or to be a pharaoh, because in Exodus Pharaoh ruled harshly and was condemned for it. It is not the jobs themselves that were condemned (Romans 13:1-7 upholds the place of authorities, and Matt 22:21 upholds the giving of taxes), but it was the way the people were carrying out the job that led to their rebuke. They failed to follow God's example of dominion. They were condemned not because their jobs were wrong, but because their actions were evil. All work is significant and must honor God.

God gives countless ways to work, and we should see the privilege of all these ways. I (the Greek teacher) used to think the job of a used car salesmen was an irredeemable position. That was until I saw Scott at work. He was a Christian who took his job seriously, and saw it as an opportunity to help others by finding the car that fit their needs. He knew his work mattered and sought to glorify God by treating customers with care and dignity, and as a result people trusted him and enjoyed working with him. He was a great example to me that a person can take an often abused position and do it with great dignity and responsibility to further God's purposes. Watching him work erased any doubt in my mind that the activity of a car salesman "touches to please God." We should view all work, even that of used car salesmen and Greek teachers, as legitimate and valued ways of pleasing God.

1.5 Called to Work

In life there are many ways to extend dominion, but that does not mean every person is suited for every job. This can be a difficult lesson to learn, and some of our deepest disappointment in work will come when we are told we are not fit for a job we really wanted. This is where firmly understanding God's calling and equipping gives faith and confidence for the jobs we do find ourselves in.

God is in the details of our life, and work is no exception. One of the subjects that stands at the forefront of understanding work is the doctrine of calling. This doctrine teaches that where we work is not by accident or mistake, but rather God assigns and calls us to specific situations (1 Cor 7:17). It shows that the jobs we take are by his design. He determines the tasks, timing, and place, and calls us to them.

In discussing calling, people have traditionally talked of two callings: a general calling and a particular calling. The general calling is the call to obey and glorify God. It is the call to live a godly life; a life dedicated to him.[12] God commands people to exercise dominion, but the most important call is the call to serve and obey him. Examples of this call are when God calls Abraham to leave everything he has and follow him (Gen 12:1), Jesus called the disciples to leave everything and follow him (Mark 1:17), and God called the apostle Paul to turn from his ways and follow him (Acts 9), so also all people are called to submit to God in faith

---

[12] Ryken, 191.

(Mark 1:15, James 4:7). General calling is about God calling all people to trust and serve him, and it reminds us that "we are not primarily called to do something... we are called to someone."[13] The primary and most important part of life, work included, is honoring and submitting to God. We are called to glorify God first and foremost, and this is the most foundational step for all of life.

In addition to the general calling to serve God is a particular calling, which is more subjective and specific to each individual person. A particular calling means God calls people to serve him in particular or specific ways. Everyone is called to serve God, but one may do this through ministry, another through sales, and another through management. God calls all people to extend dominion, and he crafts specific opportunities for people to work and serve him. Some examples of the particular calling in the Bible are Bezalel and Oholiab who were called to be craftsmen for the tabernacle (Ex 31:2), Moses who was called to lead the people out of Egypt, and David who was called to be king (1 Sam 16:1-13). Each had a specific gifting and situation the Lord put them in to serve him.

When we find ourselves in a job, or perhaps hindered from another job, we need to realize the Lord has us where we are, and we should be faithful to serve him in that position. Our being there is not by mistake or accident. Our cosmic CEO has assigned us a particular job to care for his creation, and as he has us there we can be confident there is meaningful work to do.

1.6 Gifted to Work

One key factor that influences a particular calling is the gifting God gives to people. Very often the way God calls people to a particular job is through the gifting he gives. God commands people to work, and he also blesses them to do it. The gift *of* work is accompanied by the gift *to* work. Understanding how we are gifted goes hand in hand with understanding our calling, because God often calls us to serve him in places that fit our giftings (1 Cor 7:7, Rom 12:4-8).

---

[13] Os Guiness, *The Call* (Nashville: Thomas Nelson, 2003), 45.

Each person has their own gifting, and that means some people will be better at certain jobs than others. Rather than giving into the temptation to compare our gifts with others and then lament the differences, we need to see the importance of these different giftings. William Perkins said, "If there were not different giftings then all would have the same calling, and for this reason God gives a diversity of desires inwardly and differing abilities outwardly, and so particular callings arise because of the distinction God makes between people.[14] Particular callings flow out of the mixture of different desires, giftings, and aptitudes that God gives.

These different giftings account for the many ways people extend dominion over the world. If there were not different gifts everyone would have the same job. Think of a world like that! It would be tragically boring and void of much goodness. But instead God gives different desires and gifts so that some people are butchers, some are cake makers, some are Broadway Singers, some are bookkeepers, some are elementary teachers, and some are nuclear physicists. It is the differing desires and abilities of people that lead them to different callings and unique ways to bless others.

God also gives different aptitudes for gifts. With the gift of leadership, one person may be gifted to lead a group of ten and another may be gifted to lead a group of a thousand (Exodus 18:21, 25; Deut 1:15). Two people may have a gift of management, yet one will manage a small business and another a billion dollar corporation. Both can honor God and serve others, but their different capacities may put them in very different roles. Each has a gifting with great dignity and responsibility, and each should be content to use their gifts according to the measure of gifting given to them (Romans 12:3).

It also needs to be said that God does not give us just one gift but often multiple gifts[15] and each gift with varying aptitudes. This mixture of gifts and abilities makes us proficient for a variety

---

[14] William Perkins, "William Perkings on Callings" in Edmund S. Morgan, *Puritan Political Ideas: 1558-1794,*" (Indianapolis: Hacket Publishing, 1965), 51. This is a paraphrase of a more cumbersome quote of his.

[15] Perkins, 50. Perkins speaks of several gifts as a way people are distinguished among society, which gives a hierarchical structure to society.

of works. We are each competent in many areas, above average in some, and exceptional in a few. Most jobs require more than one skill or gift, and the mixture of differing abilities can be as important as any single gift. This means that people are never locked into just one job or field but are instead equipped to do a variety of tasks and jobs as God provides opportunity. Paul was a preacher and also a tent maker. David was a shepherd and a king. The mixture of gifts God has given makes it possible to do different jobs and tasks in different seasons, and it is very likely we will experience a variety of callings in our lifetime.

Lastly, these specific giftings and particular callings are a very personal and subjective topic that all too often leads our me-centered society to think about them only in terms of self-gratification, which prevents people from seeing a more important part of their gifting. As we are called to do good to others through work, our gifting and calling makes the most sense when we view it in light of the community. We are not self-sufficient and are not made to live by ourselves. For society to more fully experience God's purposes in the world, there needs to be people with different giftings. The Bible compares the different gifts of people to the different parts of a body (1 Cor 12). A body needs hands, feet, head, and arms to function properly. We cannot say an ear or eye is unimportant. Each is vital! Likewise we must see that our variously measured gifts are to be used for the good of others (1 Cor 12:7). William Perkins said we are to use our various giftings "for the common good: that is for the benefit and good estate of mankind."[16] Just as hands, head, and feet are essential for a body to function properly, so also for the world to function properly there needs to be different people doing different jobs. Not everyone can be a doctor, or engineer, nor should they be. We need nurses, policemen, customer service reps, politicians, real estate agents, and many other professions.

Whatever gifts we have or whatever calling we find ourselves in presents an opportunity to glorify God by serving other people. It presents the opportunity to extend his purposes and do work that is truly significant. The positions we end up in are in

---

[16] Perkins, 39.

the Lord's hand and we need to be faithful to glorify him with the gifts and opportunities he gives by serving others.

God equips us for the task of extending dominion by giving various giftings and callings, and in doing so God blesses everyone with gifts to honor him by serving others. Everyone is gifted and called by God to do work that is significant and meaningful, and we should not doubt this, even when we are told our gifts are not good enough for a specific job. God gifts us for what he calls us to do.

1.7 Discovering Our Calling

We are all commanded to work and should seek after work, but how do you know the right place to apply your gifts? How do you decide to major in finance or economics, or to take one job over another? Such questions can leave people uncommitted to a specific path and drifting in a sea of uncertainty. While there is no one-size-fits-all answer to such questions, there are some things that can help us discover God's calling.

First, determining calling begins with evaluating ourselves in regards to gifting (Rom 12:6-8), desires (Ecc 3:22), opportunities (Ecc 9:10), and needs (1 Tim 5:8). Each of these plays a significant role and should be considered. A perfect job is one that we are gifted at, enjoy doing, meets our needs, and opens when we need it, but for the majority of jobs we will need wisdom and prayer to determine which of these components gets the most prominence. Each is important and should be considered in the process, but they are not always guaranteed.

Second, a gift people often neglect in evaluating these decisions is the gift of the wisdom of friends (Prov 15:22). John Frame said, "God gives to each believer wisdom to discover how God has gifted him and how he can best use that gift in God's kingdom. That wisdom should of course be compared with that of other believers, who can help us to evaluate our gifts."[17] When making decisions on work we should take advantage of those that know us and our gifts. They can provide valuable insight on how

---

[17] John Frame, *Doctrine of the Christian Life* (Phillipsburg: P&R Publishing, 2002), 312.

we may or may not fit certain positions. Hearing their input doesn't obligate us to do exactly what they say, but considering their insight on our giftings will always allow us to make a more informed decision.

Lastly, our immediate calling is not based on where we would like to be, but on where we are currently. We need not wonder where or when to begin applying this teaching on work. It is whatever situation or role the Lord currently has you in. It may be in the hunt for a job or rejuvenating your desire for a job you have been working for years. Wherever you are at and whatever you are currently doing is the place God calls you to apply his word and further his purposes. The place God has you right now is a glorious place, and you should have conviction and certainty in that place.

Finding your calling does not obligate you to stay in your current position forever, but it does demand recognition that this is where God has you and where he calls you to obedience now. Discovering our calling is a lifelong pursuit to continually evaluate as God brings various seasons of life, but the doctrine of calling should inspire faith, excitement, and conviction about the specific place God has us at the moment. No one should be sitting around thinking their job is meaningless, insignificant, or boring. Instead we need to discover the glorious opportunity that is right in front of our eyes.

1.8 Conclusion

In college, a friend of mine named James found himself in school and unmotivated to work. Each day he found something to do besides studying and going to class, and he was soon expelled for bad grades. His parents cut off financial support, and he was quickly in dire need of work. Taking the only job he could find, he started work as a brick mason, and though he had little desire for this position, he worked simply to make ends meet.

One day with no helmet on (and not following correct procedures) he was hit in the head by a brick that fell from a second story window. He felt a sharp thud on his head followed by a rush of blood over his face. It was a terrible accident, but also a pivotal moment in his career. He immediately realized he was squandering opportunities and knew he needed to change. With newfound motivation, he began to apply himself. He eventually gained re-admittance to school and went on to make honor roll all his remaining semesters.

James is a great example of what a difference the right perspective can make. He went from having little regard and excitement for his work to having a deep appreciation and much eagerness. Unfortunately, it took getting hit in the head by a brick for him to realize it.

For me, hearing the biblical teaching on work was in many ways like getting hit by a brick. It was only then that I began to see work not as a punishment but as a fundamental privilege, and also as a way to honor God and further his purposes in the world. It radically transformed my view and enjoyment of work and gave me a solid foundation to withstand the attacks of apathy. I started to see work not as a grind but a great calling where I could do things that really mattered, and I hope you are beginning to see that too.

Chapter 1 Discussion Questions

1. In what ways do you see your work suffering from a weak foundation? What biblical concepts are most helpful for you to hear?

2. How can you emulate God's good and creative purposes in your work?

3. What are the most common ways your particular profession is done the wrong way? What are you doing to make sure your work honors God?

4. What are the gifts, aptitudes, and desires that God has given you? How can you use those to serve God and people?

Chapter 2

The Right Goal—Working for True Glory

"Whatever you do, do it all for the glory of God."
1 Corinthians 10:31

As an avid sports fan, I enjoy watching almost any sporting event, but by far my favorite events are the championship games, and like many people, I watch championship games for sports I normally don't even follow. The most enjoyable part of these games is not usually the games themselves but the moments following them. It's seeing the victory celebration, and the rejoicing that comes with the crowning of a champion. It's watching the players receive their trophy in the midst of confetti falling, fans cheering, and fireworks sounding.

The celebration gets even better when a veteran player near the end of his career is interviewed. The resounding theme heard in his raspy voice is that all the hard work, the years and years of practice finally paid off. It was all "worth it." He has achieved a long time goal and is now experiencing a moment of glory—the reward for all his hard work. He and his teammates have worked with much determination toward a specific goal, and they can now say their sacrifice was worth it.

No matter how hard it is to admit the reality is very few people will ever receive a celebration like this for their work. Every now and then I like to imagine it happening to me at the office. You know where you hand in your work, and everybody turns to you in slow motion with mouths wide open and marvel in their eyes. Then the cheers, high-fives, and fireworks erupt, people begin shouting "I can't believe it," and the TV crews come asking how you were able to complete your project. Though I like to imagine this, the truth is much of our work will go unnoticed, and the lack of attention and celebration is another opportunity for us to wonder if our work matters at all.

There are two big reasons beyond just enjoying sports that I like watching championship celebrations and why I mention it here. The first is because in some ways these celebrations are a faint reminder of the greater celebration to come in heaven that will make our work "worth it." The second reason is that the perseverance, determination, and focus these athletes demonstrate in pursuing their goals remind me how I should pursue my goals, and what is more important than pursuing earthly goals in this manner is pursuing spiritual goals with the same attitude. Before we can talk about pursing goals with the right attitude, we must first make sure the right goal is clearly being pursued. For this reason we now bring the ultimate goal clearly into focus.

2.1 The Goal: The Glory of God

It is important for us to have the right goal established, because our goal directs all we do. The athlete vying for the Super Bowl championship works out every day, studies film, practices route running, and adjusts his diet all year long. His goal determines what he does each day. Likewise, our goal also determines what we do, and for that reason it is imperative to have the right goal in view, and having the right goal means our goal is God's goal for us.

The best summary of the biblical teaching on our purpose or chief end in life comes from the Westminster Confession of Faith. It concisely states, "The chief end of man is to glorify God and enjoy him forever." This confession appropriately sums up texts like 1 Cor 10:31 "So whether you eat or drink or whatever you do, do it all for the glory of God," and Romans 11:36 "For from him and through him and to him are all things. To him be the glory forever!" Isaiah 43:7 shows God made everything in creation for the purpose of bringing him glory, and Isaiah 48:11 shows God's indignation and promised retribution for those who fail to honor him saying, "For my own sake I do this. How can I let myself be defamed? I will not yield my glory to another."

The most important purpose for us is to glorify God in all we do. This is the chief goal that reigns over all other goals and the true end that everything else leads to. We are to glorify God by making him and his name great. We live to bring honor and praise to Him. This is what all of life is to be. Glorifying God is not just for pastors and clergy but is what all people are created to do.

God's chief goal in all that he made was to be glorified, and he gives this same goal to creation. God made creation to glorify him. Since people are a part of creation, that is their chief goal, and since work is something people do, the chief end of work is to glorify God. Any attempt to redefine work, or heighten our view of it, must do so by showing how it leads to this goal. The glory of work is most clearly seen in the opportunity it presents to glorify God.

The primary goal of work is not glorifying ourselves, earning six figures, winning a Super Bowl, becoming a CEO, or bettering society. It is fundamentally to glorify God and make him great, and it is imperative we get this goal right. Miroslave Volf states well this importance saying, "work is not about self-realization, the betterment of society, or the attainment of good, it is fundamentally and most elementally about the glory of God. If this goal be distorted all other goals are lost and destined to be burned up."

God's glory is our chief end and the end goal that brings all other goals into perspective. This goal gives significance and direction to our work, and if this goal is missed all other achievements are worthless. Whether working as CEO of a major corporation or a summer intern with a startup business the goal is the same—glorify God. No job is too lowly or too lofty for this chief goal, therefore all work matters, because all work is a chance to work for this chief end.

2.2 The Reward: Eternal Glory

It is important to talk briefly about the reward for our work, because rewards can transform our disposition. Sports players receive trophies that make all their training seem "worth it," and God promises us a reward that will make all our struggles "more than worth it." Scripture clearly teaches the reward God has for his people is of surpassingly greater worth than any reward on earth.

The greatness of God's reward is in fact one reason not to set our hearts on earthly glory. God's reward is of an everlasting nature whereas earthly glory is like the glory of flowers that fall and grass which withers (1 Peter 1:4, 24). The most glorious moment of the greatest athletes on the grandest stage quickly comes to an end. Their trophies will rust, stadiums will fall, their chiseled bodies will sag, and in twenty years most of their names will not be remembered, but God's glory endures forever.

The reward God offers us is to be with him forever in a new heaven and new earth where the effects of sin are no longer felt. It is to be in the greatest victory celebration ever and receive a reward whose glory will never perish, spoil, or fade (1 Pet 1:4). Receiving this unending glory will more than make up for all the labors and difficulties that are encountered on the way. As 2 Corinthians 4:17 points out, "Our light and momentary troubles are achieving for us an eternal glory that far outweighs them all." God's reward is infinitely greater than any reward or trophy the world has to offer.

2.3 The Test: God's Judgment

The reward of God is not given to everyone. When Jesus returns in his heavenly glory, "All the nations will be gathered before him, and he will separate the people one from another as a shepherd separates the sheep from the goats" (Matthew 25:32). The unrighteous will go to eternal punishment, and the righteous to eternal life (Matt 25:46).There is a great judgment coming, and the stakes are high. The reward of glory is like nothing ever seen, but the punishment is equally great.

The most fearful part of this judgment is that based on what we have done no one will be judged righteous (Rom 3:10). All people have sinned and fallen short of the glory of God (Rom 3:23). Everyone has failed at some point in the chief goal and therefore deserves eternal punishment (Rom 6:23). The good news is that Jesus Christ lived a righteous life and suffered for our sins, and he now offers us forgivenss by believing and trusting in his atoning work (Rom 3:24-35). The forgiveness of sins is the greatest thing we could ever receive. It is better than any job or bonus we might dream of. It is through Christ alone that we can have confidence to face God's judgment.

In addition to being judged for our faith in Jesus Christ, there will also be a judging of what we did in life. Herman Bavinck said in the final judgment "All the works performed by people recorded in the books before God are considered as well. Those works, after all, are expressions and products of the life that lives in the heart."[1] Part of our judgment will be based on the expression of our faith; in other words, what we have done.

An instructive parable of this judgment of works is Matthew 25:14-28. In this parable a master entrusts his servants with gifts (talents) and requires them to use these talents. One servant took the gifts, and put them to work earning more for the master. Another servant out of fear did nothing. When the master returned to judge the servants he said to the faithful servant, "Well done good and faithful servant." But to the unfaithful servant he said, "Depart from me you wicked and lazy servant" and then commanded him to be thrown outside into darkness where there will be weeping and gnashing of teeth. The parable teaches God gives us gifts to use for him, and our faithfulness to honor him with these gifts has an effect on our judgment.

A proper response to Jesus' gift of salvation is a life lived in adoration of him, and an inward compulsion to live for the one who died for us (2 Cor 5:14-15). In living for the one who died for us we desire to bring him glory and make him great in the world. This is done by faithfully using the gifts he has given us to influence the world through the expansion of his kingdom and his glory.

What we do now in life is determinative for what we hear when we stand before God. In speaking of the continuity between our work of furthering God's kingdom in this life and what is to come in the next life Anthony Hoekema says, "We must indeed be working for a better world now, our efforts in this life toward bringing the kingdom of Christ to fuller manifestation are of

---

[1] Herman Bavinck, *Holy Spirit, Church, and New Creation,* vol. 4 of *Reformed Dogmatics* (Grand Rapids: Baker Academic, 2008), 700.

eternal significance."[2] How we live and work now affects what we will hear on the Day of Judgment.

We all want to achieve greatness. We all want to work for glory, but if we want to work for eternal glory we do not seek to make ourselves great now. We seek to make God great and glorify him, so that we will hear "Well done good and faithful servant." We cannot sit around looking at our work with apathy and disinterest, thinking it doesn't matter and doing as little as possible to get by. Jesus' sacrifice should compel us to live for him, and do work that really matters. Our work is an opportunity to honor him and store up treasures in heaven. How we work now influences our eternity for good or bad, and our goal should be to do work what glorifies God. Since this is the goal we ought to be pursuing, we will now examine some common ways people miss this goal.

2.4 Missed Opportunities: Ways We Miss the Glory of God

To make sure we are on target with our chief goal we will first look at common ways people miss this goal. Though there are countless ways to miss this goal, we will look at the most common ways professing Christians do it. These main ways are by having 1) rival goals 2) short sighted goals, and 3) manipulated goals. Understanding these will help make sure we have our bearing accurately set on the chief goal, and it will help reconstruct a right understanding of work later.

It is also important to mention before exploring the ways we miss the glory of God that we do not miss what is truly at the heart of such errors. When we fail to honor God it means we value something else more than we value God, which is idolatry. Failing to glorify God is never by accident nor is it a morally neutral act. It is almost always due to the sin of idolatry (and this is the reason I devote a chapter to idolatry). With that in mind we now turn to look at ways of missing the glory of God.

---

[2] Anthony Hoekema, *The Bible and the Future* (Grand Rapids: William B. Eerdmans, 1979), 39.

2.5 Rival Goals

The glory of God is the chief end of man; the chief end means it is over and above all other ends. It is far superior to all other goals. If a goal is not the chief goal then it will be overcome by other goals—rival goals.

To be faithful with the chief goal means that we resist allowing other goals to govern us. It is all too common in work to say our chief goal is the glory of God, and yet our actions show other things are more important. We want that promotion, and it become more important than God. Or we want the approval of our boss, and what he thinks about us becomes the end all be all. We must resist the pressures to hold these things higher than the goal of glorifying God.

It is easy to say our chief goal is the glory of God, but if it truly is then there must be a demonstrable adhering to it at all times. It should always be held over and above other goals. One way our true goals are revealed is when we get constrained by other things. I compare it to when you drive home for Christmas and your goal is to see all your relatives and friends, but all of a sudden a couple unexpected visits or delays occur and you know you can't see everybody. All the sudden you have to make decision on which you will see. The same thing happens with goals in work.

For example let's say a person is in sales and needs to meet his quota to please his boss and earn a pay check. At the end of the month he needs one more deal to meet his quota, and he is meeting with a customer on the verge of signing with him, but the customer needs a problem solved that the salesman knows his product cannot fix. His actions will reveal what the most important goal is. Will he lie to achieve his goals for money and approval, or will he tell the truth and glorify God. Such constraining moments reveal which goal is most important.

The goal of honoring God should be held over and above all other goals. As the chief goal, it must take precedence in priority and importance. Just as a chief reigns over all the other people in the tribe, so also the chief goal should reign over all other goals. It should have no rivals to its throne. When it does not have the ascendency it has become inferior to a rival goal, and if it is inferior it is no longer the chief.

2.6 Shortsighted Goals

Another way we miss the chief goal is by being short sighted in our goals, or as I often call it, we develop "hamster wheel syndrome." Hamsters will run aimlessly on a wheel in a cage chasing that ever elusive treat dangling before their eyes. They are fixed on what is directly ahead and never realize they are going nowhere. Their vision is consumed by the dangling treat, and this is exactly what happens to many of us. Hit with urgent deadlines, pressing goals, or exciting projects we become blinded to anything else. Consumed by what is immediately before us we never see beyond that immediate goal.

The problem with being shortsighted often lies not in having bad goals but having goals consume and blind us. Our goal could be to get a good commission check, gain the approval of a boss, or get a promotion. All of these can be good things, but in desiring them too much the chief goal is lost. These lesser or subordinate goals should always lead toward the ultimate end goal, which is the glory of God, but instead our focus on them obstructs the chief goal.

In such a scenario one may say the goal is the glory of God, but reality shows a consuming desire for a subordinate goal, a goal that is not the ultimate end goal. The pursuit of a subordinate goal has severed the pursuit of the chief goal, and we fail to see past the lesser goals. It is illustrated below in Figure 1.

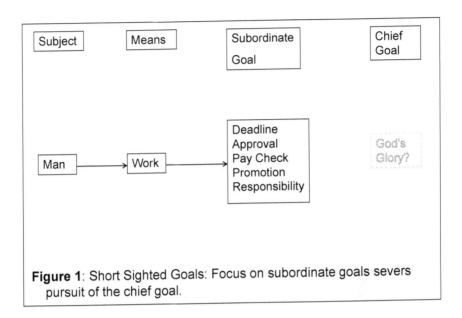

Figure 1: Short Sighted Goals: Focus on subordinate goals severs pursuit of the chief goal.

Let me explain why this is such a problem. If a representative was sent to another city to meet and get to know a certain prospective client, and after arriving there discovers there is in fact no customer in that city, the trip would be a complete failure. He may have a great time in the city seeing the sights and eating at nice restaurants, but that was not the goal. The end goal was meeting a customer. There is no reason for the trip apart from the meeting.[3] It would be absurd to call any trip a success if the very purpose of the trip was not achieved.

In the same way, it is ridiculous to think we have succeeded in gaining a promotion or greater income if these are achieved apart from glorifying God. There is no gain in achieving subordinate goals if they sever the ultimate goal. Any subordinate goal must lead to attaining the chief goal; anything else destines us for failure.

---

[3] Johnathan Edwards, *The Works of Jonathan Edwards*, vol 1 (Carlisle: Banner of Truth Trust, 1998), 95. This illustration is adapted from an illustration of Edwards.

2.7 Manipulated Goals

The third means of missing the glory of God in work is more pernicious and deceptive than the others, because it is often concealed with religion. This error not only has the wrong goals, but it often views God as a way to attain selfish goals. It's not uncommon to find a person who befriends you for a short time simply because they want something from you. It happens in elementary school, and it happens in the office. People manipulate other people for personal gain, and they also try it with God. They think that if they come to God or give him a little praise they will get what they want. John Piper describes such people saying, "If God can be seen as the enabler of their self-exaltation they will be happy to do some God-exaltation."[4] They do not see the holiness or greatness of God but instead think of him more as a genie in a bottle that if rubbed the right way can be manipulated into granting their wishes.

Manipulation of God can become even more brazen as some will "god-talk" to earn the trust of others. They will drop a line about "going to church" or utter a "praise God" if it puts them in a more favorable position. They are manipulative, and those lacking discernment may get taken advantage of.

A non-Christian small business owner once told me, "I'll never do business with anyone that talks about God while doing business. Every time somebody mentions God I end up getting screwed." In the past he had trusted people, because they talked of God (and he foolishly assumed he could trust people just because they talked about God), but in reality their talk was insincere lip-service. People who manipulate God for their own good show God is only a means and not an end to their real goals. This approach is illustrated in Figure 2 below.

---

[4] John Piper, *God is the Gospel* (Wheaton: Crossway Books, 2005), 150.

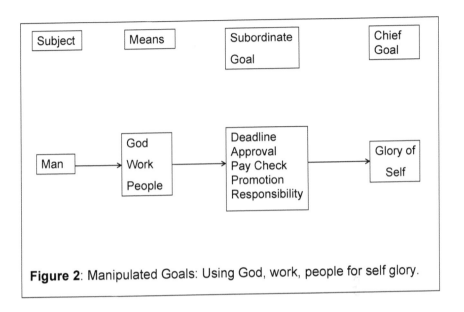

Figure 2: Manipulated Goals: Using God, work, people for self glory.

In this illustration the goal of work is distorted, because it is seen as a way for people to glorify themselves. They think life is about them getting what they want, and there is no submission to or reverence for God. God is not valued, praised, honored, nor served. Such people have no concern for him. They are hypocrites who praise God with their lips, but their hearts are far from him (Matt 15:8), and their religion is an attempt to make God worship and serve their interests. Their talk may sound pious, but in reality they view God as their servant. They must remember God said he will not be robbed of his glory.

2.8 Another Gospel

There is a major religious movement that falls in this third category, and it is known as the prosperity gospel. It has had a great influence on our culture and takes many shapes and forms. The claim of this movement is essentially "serve God and get rich" or "God wills your prosperity."[5] It appeals to people's desire to succeed materially in life and says people just need to have more faith, and they can get that new car, that bigger house, or that better job. It promises that you can have your best life now by believing and having more faith. Faith is a means to greater self-realization. God wants to bless you, but you don't experience it because you lack faith. If you would just believe and step out in faith (give to this offering, etc.) God will prosper you. Come to Jesus and get that new house, that new car, that new promotion. This may sound great, but unfortunately it simply is not biblical.

There are several major problems with this teaching. The first is that although its proponents quote the bible, they often stretch its meaning. They do this by making it appear that texts promising spiritual blessings now are talking about material possessions.[6] This mistakenly makes it appear Christ died to make us materially wealthy, which clearly contradicts the Bible.

A second major problem with the prosperity gospel is that it distorts biblical teaching by reversing the servant/Lord distinction between people and God. It teaches faith will take away our problems, which goes against many passages assuring us of difficulties in this life (Acts 14:22, 1 Peter 1:6). They also neglect passages teaching that we are to sacrifice and lay down our lives for God (Mark 10:45). They mistakenly make God and faith a means to glorify and serve ourselves. This reverses the fundamental relationship between God and people, and reduces God to the genie in a bottle or a "kind of 'cosmic bellhop' attending to our needs and desires,[7] We are to serve God because he is God, not so he will serve us, and there are severe consequences for confusing these.

---

[5] Gordon Fee, *The Disease of the Health and Wealth Gospels* (Costa Mesa CA: Agora Ministries, 1979), 1.

[6] This problem, particularly in regards to Gal 3:14 is explained very well in David Jones, "The Bankruptcy of the Prosperity Gospel: An Exercise in Biblical Theological Ethics," n.p. (cited 19 Nov 2009). Online: http://bible.org/article/bankruptcy-prosperity-gospel-exercise-biblical-and-theological-ethics.

[7] James R. Goff, Jr., "The Faith That Claims," *Christianity Today,* vol. 34, (February 1990), 21.

Understanding this errant way of viewing God can help reveal our true goals in life and if we are seeking to serve him or ourselves. In 2010 the Buffalo Bill's wide receiver Steve Johnson dropped what would have been a game winning touchdown. The ball hit his hands and fell to the ground. After the game Johnson tweeted "I PRAISE YOU 24/7!!!!!! AND THIS HOW YOU DO ME!!!!!"

This is a sad comment reflecting the feeling that because he praised God he deserved something. His statements imply God owed him something for his actions. This is a bold statement that even though we may not express verbally, we often feel it. We think, "God I went to church, I gave to that offering, I did everything right, and so I should have gotten that deal? I served you. Why didn't everything go my way?" In these times we must remember that we do not serve God to get what we want. We serve him because he is God and deserves to be glorified in everything.

The prosperity gospel strikes out in its biblical theology, but it does raise important questions related to work and blessings that we must talk about, and that is: What should we make of the biblical texts proponents of the prosperity gospel often use like "ask and it will be given to you; seek and you will find" (Luke 11:9) and "All hard work brings a profit" (Prov 14:23). After all, doesn't Jesus promise to meet our needs and doesn't the bible give us a pattern of wisdom for succeeding in the world?

The answers to these are yes. The Bible does give us wisdom to succeed in life, and it does teach that Jesus hears our prayers. It is biblical that if one trusts in God and seeks to apply God's word their lives will be blessed and enriched spiritually and materially (Psalm 1, 1 Cor 1:5). While there often appears a connection between biblical faith and material success, the connection is, as Gordon Fee says, "not a one thing in exchange for another."[8] In other words the connection is not do this and this and you will get this (it's not go to church, give to this, and you get _____).

The connection between faith and material success is more like a nexus. There is a connection, but it is not a mathematical connection. It is more like the connection of character and success.

---

[8] Fee, 6.

Those with good character *usually* succeed (Psalm 1:3), and those who sow good *usually* reap it (Gal 6:7). It is a general principal with exceptions, so that it cannot be manipulated for gain. It is an intricate nexus where things are related but the connection is not always clear.[9] Scripture is content to show the reaping of what is sown comes imprecisely in "due season" (Gal 6:9, ESV), and it firmly rejects any ability to manipulate God for results.

We must see that any attempt to serve or manipulate God for personal prosperity will result in failure to the chief goal and potential loss of his incomparable reward. Gustave Aulen warned,

> Every attempt to transform Christian faith into a religion of satisfaction and enjoyment is thereby doomed to failure. Egocentricity masquerading in the robes of religion is excluded. Faith in God cannot be measured and evaluated from the point of view of human happiness and needs, even if these concepts be ever so refined and "spiritualized." ... Every tendency to make God serve human interests is irrevocably doomed.[10]

The prosperity gospel distorts biblical teaching and feeds the craving of sinful people to see God as a means to satisfy carnal cravings. It misunderstands the connections of God, faith, work, and success. It distorts our chief end and offers an alternative understanding of faith for success that is hollow and deceptive. When people come to Christ their life is enriched, but they must resist thinking that by doing certain things God is obligated to prosper them. God desires his people to value and worship him above everything else, not that they worship him in order to increase their material wealth. Such thinking makes God the means of worshiping our idols and is doomed to failure.

---

[9] Bruce Waltke, *The Book of Proverbs,* vol 1, NICOT (Grand Rapids: William B. Eerdmans Publishing Company, 2005), 73-76.
[10] Gustave Aulen in Fee, 9-10.

2.9 A Positive Reconstruction of Work

After setting forth various incorrect ways to pursue work, a positive reconstruction needs to be given. One that sees the importance of work as a means to achieve the very end we were created for. Such a reconstruction should also account for immediate goals, but show them as clearly subordinate to the chief goal. This reconstruction is shown below.

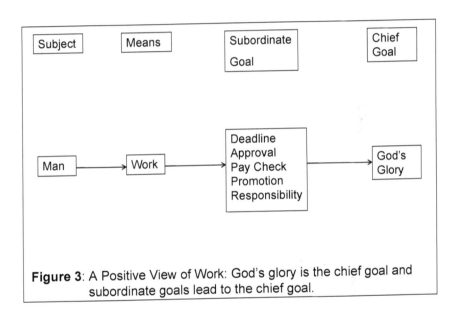

Figure 3: A Positive View of Work: God's glory is the chief goal and subordinate goals lead to the chief goal.

This diagram is not perfect, nor is it complete, but it is helpful for several reasons. First, it shows the chief most important goal is God's glory, and that stands unrivaled as the ultimate end goal. Secondly, it shows the vital place of subordinate goals. We need to achieve things like paychecks if we are to honor God. I am a father of four and my wife stays at home. I am acutely aware of the need to provide, and this diagram shows these goals, but reminds they are to be done in a way that leads to the chief goal.

While this diagram is helpful, a weakness is that it doesn't show how work and subordinate goals actually create opportunities to glorify God. It is important to not just connect work and God's glory, but to see how dominion creates opportunities to honor God. God created people to rule over his creation for his glory, therefore all creation is a platform to stand on as a means of glorifying God. John Murray best states this saying,

> When we remember that the ultimate goal of man's creation and endowment, and the creation and endowment of the earth as the sphere and platform of his employment, was not the cultivation of his powers and cultivation of the earth's resources for the promotion of his (man's) own good and enjoyment, but the magnifying of God's glory, then a vista of frontiers and employments opens to our vision.[11]

Work appropriately understood is a means for people to use their gifts to extend dominion over creation, and the various forms of dominion are platforms to stand on to bring God glory. Work creates opportunities to influence the world by expanding God's kingdom and glory. The best reconstruction of work would show work creating a frontier of opportunities to glorify God, and is illustrated below.

---

[11] John Murray, *Principals of Conduct* (Grand Rapids: Eerdmans, 1957), 37.

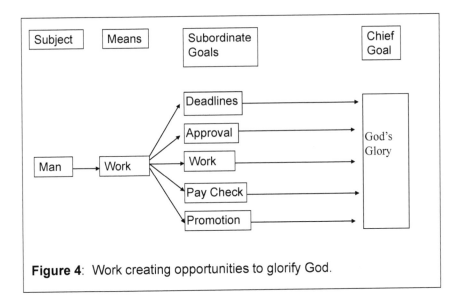

Figure 4: Work creating opportunities to glorify God.

When properly seen subordinate goals are not simply ends in themselves, but another means of bringing God glory. As one works and receives an income, a new means of glorifying God is created by honoring him with money. It is a new opportunity to further his kingdom, give to his causes, and show the world we desire to make him great. The same is true of paychecks, promotions, projects, deadlines, and everything else we do. These create avenues for doing work that spreads God's glory.

In addition, as one is faithful to what God has given, it usually opens up increased opportunities of influence. A person who progressively succeeds in his job may soon be asked to manage a small group of people, then a department, and then possibly an entire company. Another may gain more penetrating influence where they go from enforcing policies to writing policies, or perhaps they gain deepening influence with others like a teacher does as he gets to know his students. This means their sphere of influence is increasing. It is effectively going from

$$o \rightarrow O \rightarrow O$$

As our sphere of dominion increases, it increases the effect we can have on shaping the world for the glory of God. With increased dominion we have increased potential to do more good and effect more people for the glory of God.

This understanding of work shows that the desire to succeed in work or achieve a promotion is not bad and in fact can channel efforts to doing great things for the chief goal. When we understand God's gift of dominion and the call to glorify him we begin to see that we can do work that really matters. Work is not an irrelevant unglorious part of life, but rather a profound opportunity to honor God and influence the world.

2.10 The Effects of Working for the Glory of God

New goals can change people dramatically. A person on a diet packs a smaller lunch, is annoyingly aware of how many calories are in all foods, and gives you condescending looks when you ask them to go to the Chinese buffet. Their goal affects their inner attitudes and external actions. If superficial goals like diets have great effects, how much more should the goal of "working for the Lord and not for men" (Col 3:23) have a vast array of effects on our attitudes and actions. We have established our chief goal, and we now look at some specific effects that goal should have on our work.

We work with all our heart. If the president of our company were to ask us to do a direct assignment for him, we probably wouldn't do it half-heartedly. It is only natural that if all our work is done for the CEO of the universe then our work should be done with all we have. Jonathan Edwards said, "Wherever true religion is, there are vigorous exercises of the inclination and will."[12] Our faith that everything is done for God's glory should stir us to work with physical vigor and heartfelt affection. And as Edwards says

---

[12] Jonathan Edwards, *Religious Affections* (Edinburgh: Banner of Truth Trust, 1997), 29.

again, "These affections are the springs that set men a-going in all the affairs of life."[13] Seeing God as the one to whom work is done for will set our hearts on fire for work (and many other things in life). Everything we do is done for Him, and therefore we do everything with all our might. This internal attitude is what drives all that we do.

We work with all our heart in whatever we do. Our passion is not reserved only for the enjoyable parts of work but extends to *whatever* we do, including the difficult and disliked parts. We work wholeheartedly for the harsh boss, for the demeaning tasks, the unfair assignments, monotonous projects, and even the jobs we wish would end soon. John Murray has a helpful reminder for us on this,

> When labor involves drudgery, when hardship is oppressive, when the conditions imposed upon us are not those which mercy and justice would dictate, when we are tempted to individual and organized revolt, when we are ready to recompense evil on the part of our master with the evil of careless work on our part, it is just then that we need to be reminded, "whatsoever you do, do it heartily as to the Lord and not to men, knowing that from the Lord you shall receive the recompense of the inheritance."[14]

We do all things wholeheartedly, because we know God will reward us, and we know all these circumstances are opportunities to work for the chief end.

We work with God-honoring conduct. We are not concerned simply with the results of work. "We do the Lord's work in the Lord's way."[15] It is not appropriate to just be content with getting a promotion. It means how we get the promotion matters. Working for God's glory brings new ethical standards. Work is no longer about just money or bottom line figures, but honoring him. There is to be integrity in all of life including what

---

[13] Edwards, 29.
[14] Murray, 87.
[15] Francis Shaffer quoted in Darrow Miller, *Lifework* (Seattle: YWAM, 2009), 321.

we do in private, because everything is done in full view of our boss (Prov 5:21) and we want to honor him.

We work with a steady eye to God's word. We cannot honor God if we do not know what God-honoring conduct looks like. We must be in God's word daily, holding our life to his word, and diligently seeking to conform to it. As William a' Brakel said, "Continually hold this law before you as being the will of God; approve of it, obediently subject yourself to it… and keep it in view as a carpenter does his blueprint."[16] If a carpenter tosses away his blue print to a house he will soon begin to improvise and adjust the construction of the house. It is a matter of time before the house's features are distorted to something not intended. As a carpenter consistently looks to the blue prints to guide his work, so also we must consistently look to God's word to guide our life.

We work with excellence. After God formed the world he stood back and evaluated what he had done, and saw his work was good (Gen 1:10, 12, 18, 21, 25), and we too must do good. Those who do things poorly show a separation between them and their work. "A worker who is indifferent to what he is making and to how his product is made is estranged from his work"[17] and from God. Those who see the connection between their work and serving God will not only do their work with an attitude worthy of the Lord, but will also produce a finished product worthy of him. Dorothy Sayers strongly exhorts people to produce quality work in what they do saying, "No crooked table-legs or ill-fitted drawers ever, I dare swear, came out of the carpenters shop in Nazareth."[18] She then goes on to say "The only Christian work is good work well done."[19] The importance of good work well done cannot be overstated. No false piety or hollow statements of serving God in vocation will stand when shoddy work is done. People should see our work and give thanks to God.

---

[16] Wilhelmus a' Brakel, *The Christian's Reasonable* Service, vol 3, translated by Bartel Elshout, edited by Joel Beeke (Grand Rapids: Reformation Heritage Books, 2007), 81.

[17] Volf, 200.

[18] Dorothy Sayers, *Creed or Chaos*, (New York: Harcourt, Brace and Company, 1949), 57.

[19] Ibid, 58.

We work for influence. It's not enough to be content to monitor our internal attitudes or assess the quality of our work without going after external influence. We seek to bring good to the world and that includes persuading others of the need to live for the glory of God (2 Cor 5:11). We want them to know of the coming judgment and the provision of a Savior. We want others to know it is what this Savior has done that gives meaning to our work and drives our internal attitudes and external actions. We want them to know the true chief goal in life and how all other goals should be subservient to this goal. We want to glorify God by telling others he is what deserves to be supreme in life.

We work where we can glorify God. This needs to be approached with caution, because we do not want work to be the end all be all of our responsibility before God. There may be times we take a less demanding job to focus on family or another particular responsibility, but often decisions for work are made based on how much we like the work, amount of income, days of vacation, where we get to live, or what school the kids could attend. These have a role to play, but how often does one say, "The biggest factor is finding the place that I can most influence the world for God's glory." Understanding our chief goal should lead us to ask this question. Gary Badcock said, "The values of the kingdom must inform and even determine the shape of Christian vocation."[20] For disciples of Christ, it is a moral failure to not let the values of the kingdom inform our career choice.[21] Failing to consider our career in light of our chief goal shows a rival may already be enthroned.

2.11 Conclusion

Most of us will not have the privilege of being center stage for elite sports celebrations, but that should not tempt us to think our work doesn't matter or we don't have a great reward in store. Jesus Christ's atoning death for sin has made a way for us to

---

[20] Gary D. Badcock, *The Way of Life* (Grand Rapids: Eerdmans, 1998), 52.

[21] Ibid. This is a paraphrase of Badcock.

41

receive the greatest prize, and his death compels us to glorify God in all we do. We now have the opportunity in all we do to work for the grandest goal, the highest calling, and the greatest reward—the glory of God. It is this goal we seek after above all others, and it this goal that guides our internal thoughts and external actions. In our work we are indeed working for glory, but the ironic twist is that it is not our glory we are primarily concerned with but the glory of God. When we focus on this goal all work becomes a means to achieve it, and that means we have the opportunity to gain a glory that far surpasses anything the world has to offer.

Chapter 2 Discussion Questions

1. How does the death and resurrection of Jesus connect to and motivate you to work on a daily basis?

2. What most commonly causes you to miss working for God's glory? How do you fight against that?

3. Are you ever tempted to serve God just to get what you want? What is wrong with this thinking?

4. What can you do to advance God's glory through your work? What can you do to deepen and widen your influence?

Chapter 3

The Mission— Work as Ministry

*"The LORD God took the man
and put him in the Garden of Eden
to work it and take care of it."
Genesis 2:15*

Rob had been working with a commercial printing business for several years and was well on his way to becoming a successful partner with the company. One evening after work, he and his family attended church to hear a missionary speak about ministering to a third world country. That night Rob listened intently as the missionary told thrilling stories about repairing villages, healing illnesses, and sharing the gospel, so that entire tribes were putting their faith in Jesus. It was one exciting testimony after another, and Rob was stirred to advance the gospel.

Immediately after the meeting, he went and talked to the missionary and shared how his heart was stirred for missions, and how he now hoped that one day he might retire early or get the business to a point where he could pull away and then get involved in missions. After hearing Rob share his desires, the missionary turned to him and sternly said, "You already are in missions. You are in it every day you go to work. You just need to realize it." Rob was struck by these words and began wondering if he was missing opportunities right in front of him. He was a little perplexed but nonetheless provoked to advance the gospel at work.

He began praying about this and seeking opportunities at work to share with others. After few days his boss asked him to meet in his office. Rob was excited and thought this could be the opportunity he hoped for. Rob eagerly came to his office and sat down, and that's when his boss began to tell him he was behind on his quota and if he didn't get his backside to work he would be looking for another job! Now Rob was even more confused about his work and the mission. He thought there was a connection but also realized it was more complex than he initially thought.

No doubt many can relate to Rob's confusion. The mission God gives us to advance his purposes in the world should connect to our work but that connection needs balancing. If we don't have a right understanding of this we will either neglect part of the mission or part of the reason God has us at work, and to do either of these misses the point, and if we don't find sound answers to this it can leave us sitting on the job (or unemployed) wandering if our work matters at all. To solve this problem we now turn to a passage that helps us understand the connection of work and ministry.

3.1 Work in the Garden.

Genesis 1 provides the foundation for work, and the very next chapter of Genesis shows the relation of ministry and work. Genesis 2:15 says, "The LORD God took the man and put him in the Garden of Eden to work it and take care of it." Adam is called to tend a garden, but this garden is much more than an ordinary garden, and understanding this is key to rightly viewing work.

There are many unique things in this garden. It is a plush place where life flourishes. It is beautifully decorated with trees pleasing to the eye and good for food (Gen 2:9), gold is in abundance (2:11-12), and the aroma is pleasant (2:12). Even its name "Eden" means pleasurable or delightful. Its puts our greatest beach resorts to shame. But the most unique thing about this garden is that it is the place God walks with people (3:8). God uniquely meets with his people here, which leads us to see this garden is a temple, and a temple that all later temples and tabernacles pattern themselves after. Speaking of the garden in this way, Bruce Waltke says,

> It represents territorial space in the created order where God invites human beings to enjoy bliss and harmony between themselves and God, one another, animals, and the

land. God is uniquely present here. The Garden of Eden is a temple-garden, represented later in the tabernacle.[1]

God meets with people in this garden in an intimate way that prefigures the tabernacle, Solomon's temple, and the final temple in Revelation. Several additional themes further develop this connection. First, God walks in Eden as he does in later temples (Lev 26:12, 2 Sam 7:6-7, Rev 21:3). Second, Eden and later temples are entered from the east and guarded by angelic creatures (Gen 3:24, Ex 25:18-22; 1 Kings 6:23-29). Third, the tabernacle lampstand likely symbolizes the tree of life (Gen 2:9, Ex 25:31-35, Rev 22:2). Fourth, the river flowing from Eden is reminiscent of the river bringing life in Ezekiel and Revelation (Ezek 47:1-12, Rev 22:2). Fifth, gold and onyx are used extensively to decorate later sanctuaries (Ex 25:7, 11, Rev 21:18).[2] The garden was a temple, and it is in that garden-temple Adam would work.

Another key theme connecting the garden and the temple is the language used for Adam's work, and this theme brings the passage to bear on our work. In Genesis 2:15 the word "work" (aved) means to cultivate or serve someone, and the words for "take care" (shamar) means to watch over or guard. These words show they were to build up and protect the garden, but the most significant point about these two words in the expression "work it and take care of it" is that the words only occur together in reference to the duties of priests.[3] From the use of these words it can be concluded that Adam in his work is being portrayed as a priest.[4] He was to cultivate this garden to be a holy place.

Adam and Eve as priests were to build and protect the temple of God, and their calling as priests combined with the cultural mandate (Gen 1:28) implies they were created to work in the garden, and through dominion and reproduction were to expand the garden throughout the entire earth. Connecting this work in the

---

[1] Bruce Waltke, *Genesis,* (Grand Rapids: Zondervan, 2001), 85.

[2] T.D. Alexander, *From Paradise to Promise Land* (Grand Rapids: Baker Academic, 2002), 131.

[3] Waltke, *Genesis*, 87.

[4] G. K. Beal, *The Temple and the Church's Mission* (NSBT 17; Downers Grove: Intervarsity Press, 2004), 81.

garden with the cultural mandate Gregg Beal says, "Because Adam and Eve were to subdue and rule 'over all the earth,' it is plausible to suggest that they were to extend the boundaries of the garden until Eden covered the whole earth."[5] They were to make the entire earth a garden, or temple of the Lord. Pursuit of the cultural mandate should be seen as a process of temple building, because God formed the world as his cosmic temple."[6]

The garden-sanctuary as the place God dwells with his people along with the abundance of life and goodness in it presents this garden as the centre of world blessing,[7] and Adam and Eve through their work were to expand this delightful sanctuary from a confined area until it covered the entire earth. Adam and Eve were put in the garden to work and cultivate a beautiful place where there would be no evil and God's special presence would dwell, with the intent that through their obedient dominion the entire earth would become God's temple.

Expanding the dwelling of God throughout the earth would entail cultivating good, driving out evil, and furthering the kingdom of God. This calling also has much to do with the great commission to "Go and make disciples of all nations, baptizing them in the name of the Father and of the Son and of the Holy Spirit" (Matt 28:18-19). Again Bruce Waltke says,

> The great commission to baptize all nations in the name of the Father, Son, and Holy Spirit and the cultural mandate complement, not compete against, each other. God's irrupting kingdom in a world that needs taming entails a people who purpose to develop a culture that pleases him. The Westminster Catechism teaches that "the chief end of man is to glorify God and enjoy him forever," but it needs to be clarified that humanity glorifies God by subduing the earth by words and by work.[8]

---

[5] Beal, 81-82.

[6] Meredith Kline, *Kingdom Prologue* (Overland Park: Two Ages Press, 2000), 89.

[7] William Dumbrell, *Covenant and Creation* (Mt. Radford: Paternoster, 1984), 35.

[8] Bruce Waltke, *An Old Testament Theology* (Grand Rapids: Zondervan, 2006), 221.

There is a clear connection between work and ministry, between the cultural mandate and great commission. This provides the beginning framework of the priesthood of all believers (Exodus 19:5, 1 Peter 2:5, 9) and helps us see the interconnection of work and ministry. As people were created for dominion, dominion is now qualified with a priestly aspect by which they are to labor at expanding the temple of God. This expansion includes work and words, and it seeks transformation of people and the world.

The imagery of the garden in Genesis 2 further explains our purpose in life and connects work and ministry by showing we are to labor at making the entire earth God's temple. We will now look at several ways this garden paradigm informs how work can be seen as ministry and lead toward God's goal for the world.

3.2 Ministry of Common Grace

Ministry can take many forms, but it typically involves serving people or meeting the needs of others. God has given everyone gifts to serve others with, and by serving others we administer the grace of God (1 Peter 4:10). William Perkins articulated this importance in work saying, "The main end of our lives is to serve God in the serving of men in the works of our callings."[9] He exhorts people to use their gifting "for the common good: that is for the benefit and good estate of mankind."[10] Perkins shows that using our gifts is a way to serve others for the common good (1 Cor 12:7), and I want to show that using our gifts to serve others through work is a way to bring the goodness, beauty, and delightfulness of the garden to others.

Extending this goodness is extending what many call common grace. "Common grace is the grace of God by which he gives people innumerable blessings that are not part of salvation. The word 'common' implies something that is common to all

---

[9] William Perkins, "William Perkins on Callings" in Morgan, Edmund S. *Puritan Political Ideas: 1558-1794,*" (Indianapolis: Hacket Publishing, 1965), 57.
[10] Ibid, 39.

people and is not restricted to believers."[11] Running water and pleasing food are things that come to us as God's grace and to which we give him thanks. They are good things that better life and are experienced by believers and unbelievers alike. They are not directly tied to salvation, but they do enhance life, and God repeatedly shows an interest in the quality of life we have. It would have been enough to be with God in the garden, but he provided beautiful trees, gold, good fruit, and much more. It would have been enough to have a Promised Land, but God made it flow with milk and honey (Num 13:27). Jesus could have just forgiven sins, but he also healed people (Mark 2:9-12). God's grace enhances lives by meeting needs, and our work also provides ways to extend this grace.

People frequently think of ministry solely as preaching and neglect to see the important part of practically caring for people. The qualitative aspect of ministry implied in common grace does not necessarily involve the preaching of the gospel or the sharing of God's word verbally, but rather it involves serving others by enhancing their lives. This is the larger portion of ministry a person does at the office. It is doing work for the betterment of the earth and one's neighbor.

The basis of common grace in ministry is seen in Genesis 2:15 where God meets with people in the garden. People are called to further this temple area, and the beauty and order of the garden are inescapably tied to it. Bringing beauty and form to the earth is exactly what God began doing to the world in Genesis 1 and what he completes in Revelation 22. Adam and Eve were to share in that task by laboring to make the earth the delightful place God intends it to be.

We are to labor now for what the end will be, and this involves confronting "the formless and disordered places of our world, and of our lives, and making them places of beauty and goodness."[12] It is spreading the delightfulness of the garden

---

[11] Wayne Grudem, *Systematic Theology* (Grand Rapids: Zondervan, 1994), 657.

[12] David Atkinson, *Genesis 1-11*, (Downers Grove, IL: Inter-Varsity Press, 1990), 62. Atkinson shows God's pattern for this world is not merely functional but also "pleasant to the sight" and these provide an enriching, beautifying, and life enhancing effect. See also Matt 26:10.

through the cultivation of what is good and pleasing and the restraint of what is evil and disdainful. This is the goal of common grace in work. A police officer who arrests thieves is making the world a better place by restraining evil and promoting good. Sanitation workers serve the community by removing what is disdainful and making neighborhoods pleasant places. The web designer makes sure the interface of a company is pleasant for customers and protected from thieves.

Enhancing life by restraining evil and cultivating good is a main component of work and a primary way of ministering to others and influencing the world. This passage in Genesis is the seminal basis of verses that command seeking the good of cities (Jer 29:7) and how cities also flourish when the righteous prosper (Prov 11:10). There is a connection between one realizing what God has done and what they should do.

Extending common grace is a way of doing good to the world, and just as God created a good world and did not forsake it, even after sin entered it, but instead chose to work with it and to redeem his creation, so also we should work to redeem the world by continuing to do good. It is here the gospel rightly understood should motivate us in the task of extending common grace. Alister McGrath said,

> To be Christian thus does not—indeed cannot—mean renouncing the world; for to renounce the world is to renounce the God who so wondrously created it; …. The world, though fallen, is not evil. The Christian is called to work in the world, in order to redeem the world. Commitment to the world is a vital aspect of the working out of the Christian doctrine of redemption. A failure to commit oneself to and work in the world is (equal) to declaring that it cannot, and should not, be redeemed.[13]

If people do not work to better the world it is difficult to think they take seriously the redemption of the world. We should work to redeem the world by cultivating good and restraining evil.

---

[13] Alister McGrath, *Reformation Thought* (Oxford: Blackwell Publishing, 1999), 265.

By doing so, we minister to others and connect the doctrine of creation and redemption to our everyday lives.

3.4 The Significance of Common Grace

Extending common grace is the majority of what we do in work, and it is the benefit others expect from us. Cotton Mather said "God has made man a societal creature. We expect benefits from human society. It is but equal that human society should receive benefits from us."[14] When we work with others or agree to have others work for us we expect to gain something from it. We expect them in some way to enrich our life with a service they perform. Work is a means to enhance lives by solving problems with the gifts we have been given. When my car breaks I take it to my mechanic so he can help me with something I am completely inept at. He serves me by taking what is broken and putting it back in working order. In return I gladly pay him for his work. Both of our lives are enhanced through work, and we both benefit. My car is in working order, and he can feed his family.

Common grace is also extended to employees and employers. Companies need people to fill certain positions in order to extend goodness to their customers. People are employed for a reason and faithfulness to the job is a way to extend common grace to one's employer. Employers extend common grace to their employees by providing good work and fair wages. Peoples' dependence on one another illustrates the all-encompassing nature of common grace in work.

Unfortunately many people miss the importance of common grace. When complemented for the hard work of repairing the car my mechanic often says, "I'm just doing my job." I appreciate his humility but I think the significance of what he has done gets lost. It is important to see this clearly because cultivating good and restraining evil can have a profound effect. Moral failure to extend the order and beauty of the garden is what causes evils in the world. John Rushdoony said, "Man's effort is required to cultivate the garden and the earth, and man's moral incompetence

---

[14] Leland Ryken, *Worldly Saints* (Grand Rapids: Zondervan, 1990), 23.

to image God's dominion means that the earth slips into disorder."[15] All one has to do to see the importance of common grace is look at the disorder and destruction caused by peoples' moral failings. Mechanics lie about something being broken on the car, financial advisors create schemes to rob people of life-saving, and companies profit off faulty products. In light of such moral failures, we should see the importance of extending common grace and look for opportunities to minister to the world by cultivating good and restraining evil, even in the seemingly common ways.

One person who saw the connection of common grace and ministry is William Wilberforce, whose story was told in the movie *Amazing Grace.* With a brilliant future ahead in politics, God began working on his heart, and he began to contemplate if he was called to the life of a political activist or to the ministry of the word, or as a condescending friend would say, "Are you going to use your beautiful voice to praise God or change the world?"

After much contemplation Wilberforce realized the answer was yes. He was called to both, and he fervently sought to glorify God through a career in politics. His political activities were opposed by many, but they were also the very catalyst that brought an end to slave trade in Europe and spared innumerable lives from the deep pain and destructive evil of slavery. The driving force of his work was to pass laws that would eradicate activities of society that were offensive to God.[16] His work of extending common grace restrained evil in significant ways and changed an entire nation.

Not everyone will have the opportunity to influence nations like Wilberforce, but every person has some opportunity through their work to oppress evil and do good even if it is simply building a sound product, ensuring fairness in the workplace, or confronting people taking advantage of customers. Common grace provides opportunity to do work that really matters and can be a powerful means of ministering to a world so often hurt by the sinful acts of others.

---

[15] Rousas John Rushdoony, *Institutes of Biblical Law: Law and Society,* Vol 2 (Vallecito, CA: Ross House Books, 1986), 315.

[16] John Piper, *Amazing Grace in the Life of William Wilberforce* (Wheaton: Crossway, 2006), 16.

3.5 Common Grace as a Foundation for the Gospel

We will now look at common grace and ministry in perhaps a more familiar way, but the reason for delaying this is because it is important to first see that extending common grace glorifies God and is good in and of itself. It blesses others and advances God's desire for the world. Now we turn to see common grace as a foundation for the ministry of the word.

Common grace is like the foundation of concrete that a builder lays for a house, so he can then effectively build stable walls. If we fail in common grace no one will care about our faith. It is the common grace of blessing others through work well done that forms the foundation that a credible, caring, and effective testifying of faith can be built on. God's common grace provides the opportunity for saving grace,[17] and our extension of common grace provides a basis for us to share God's word.

My church regularly sends a medical missions team to a church in India with the goal of practically serving people by providing free medical help. The hope is that in a region staunchly opposed to the gospel many who would not come to church might be opened to the gospel by having their needs met. The love of the team was demonstrated in acts of serving, and those they served inevitably asked why they would travel around the world to care for them. The team's work led to opportunities for them to share about their hope in Christ. This is what common grace can lead to, and what we should seek after.

My friend Brian was a great example of this. He was an agent providing health insurance for aging people, and his commitment to serving people provided many opportunities to share his faith. His great care and concern for his clients was seen in his detailed questions and tireless work ethic to find the best solution for their needs. Brian would usually wait for people to ask before he shared his faith, but opportunities frequently came up

---

[17] Abraham Kuyper, *A Centinial Reader*, edited by James D. Bratt (Grand Rapids: William B. Eerdmans, 1998), 169. Kuyper says common grace presupposes special grace and that common grace provides conditions which the church can take root in society.

because people felt his deep care and genuine concern through his work. Clients saw how much he cared for them and would ask why he treated them so well. In these times he would tell them he knew how to love others because Christ first loved him. After seeing his sincere care, many opened up to hearing about his faith and listened attentively. His commitment to bless people through the common grace of selling insurance provided a foundation for him to compellingly share the gospel. Like Brian we too should see the important place common grace plays in sharing our faith.

3.6 Ministry of the Word

In Genesis, Adam and Eve should have trusted God's word and resisted Satan, but instead they sinned and were themselves driven from the garden and the presence of God.[18] Their failure in work was a failure with God's words. If we are going to be successful in work we must be faithful with God's word. If we hope to advance God's mission, his word is an absolute necessity, because a saving knowledge of Christ only comes by rightly understanding God's word.

John Calvin said, "God bestows the actual knowledge of himself upon us only in the scriptures."[19] While a ministry of common grace is probably the majority of ministry that takes place in work, it cannot be the sole means of ministry. Sharing the word makes explicit what is often implicit in common grace. It is only through God's word that we come to know his salvation and can explain to others God's holiness, our sinfulness, Christ's work, and the proper response to it.

The goal of ministry is to expand the presence of God, and the presence of God is expanded by people believing in the gospel of Jesus Christ. This is the ministry we labor for most supremely. While common grace certainly blesses people, the greatest change does not come through better circumstances, newer technologies,

---

[18] Kenneth Matthews, *Genesis 1-11:26,* New American Commentary. (Nashville: Broadman and Holman Publishers, 2002), 210.

[19] John Calvin, *Institutes*, edited by John T. McNeil and translated by Ford Lewis Battles (Louisville: Westminster John Knox Press, 1960), 1.6.1.

reformed governement, or healthier bodies, but through faith in the gospel of Jesus Christ. The gospel creates the greatest transformation by setting people free from guilt, renewing the heart, and restoring the right relationship of man to God.[20]

Faith in the gospel is what we most desire, because it is a reordering of the heart to God. The gospel meets our greatest need— the forgiveness of our sins, and it gives hope in every difficulty. God's word teaches how to bring every aspect of life in line with the gospel. It teaches us how to be saved and how to rightly live in the world.

Like common grace, sharing God's word also cultivates good and restrains evil (2 Tim 3:16). Faith in the gospel is the greatest act of cultivating good and restraining evil, and it comes only by hearing God's word. These two forms of ministry have similar goals, and they also have similar entry points. Sharing God's word at work can effectivly be done by focusing on helping others.

When someone is not working as they should, has a bad attitude toward a project, is experinecing personal issues that are affecting their work, we have an opportunity to speak to better their lives. Difficulties at work are often related to deeper heart issues that revolve around sin. An effective leader can show a person where he is falling short and also what he needs to put on to overcome that, and a Christian should have a deeper understanding about these heart issues because of their knowledge of God's word. This can turn instances of hardship or poor performance into oppportunities of heart reordering ministry. When work is seen as an opportunity to shepherd people clear opportunities for ministry develop. Helping people with practical issues may start out more like extending common grace, but in doing so avenues to the heart are opened.

Brad managed a team that trained new hires for his company. He was convinced of the importance of God's word, and thought he could better his team by appropriately sharing it with them. He would regualrly meet with each member of his team to

---

[20] Herman Bavink, *Essays on Religion, Science, and Society*, edited by John Bolt and translated by Harry Boonstra and Gerrit Sheeres (Grand Rapids: Baker Academic, 2008), 142.

talk through any performance issues they had. He would help them through their weaknesses and when appropriate share verses or ideas from the bible to help them. When bigger issues surfaced he would ask to take them to lunch in order to talk more openly and personally. He humbly offered advice and recommendations of what helped him when he expereinced similar difficulties, and he would make a point to explain how God's word and his hope in Christ informed him in those times. As a result of Brad's leadership, many people on his team became more productive workers, but more importantly, through Brad's counsel some even came to know Christ as their Lord and Savior.

Everyone has opportunities to influence those they work with. As we converse with others on how to complete a job or see people struggling with issues on or off the job, we have great opportunities to help them by sharing God's word with them. It is an opportunity to help them by pointing them to a Savior who offers to reorder their lives from the inside out.

3.6 Ministry through the Fruit of Work

A third ministry opportunity in work comes from the fruit of work. God intends there to be a reward for cultivating the earth, which is evidenced in God telling Adam he could eat of all but one tree in the Garden (Gen 2:16). It was God's design for people to live off their work, and the benefit of doing work is enjoying the fruit of it.

This concept of benefiting from and providing through work is taught in many other passages. 2 Thessalonians 3:10 says "If a man will not work, he shall not eat." Proverbs 12:11 reminds that, "He who works h is land will have abundant food." Those who do not work and fail to provide for their family are considered to deny the faith and be worse than unbelievers (1 Tim 5:8).

Profiting from labor is a clear biblical concept and cannot be overlooked, especially in an age where work is not always so closely tied to the physical ground. Pope John Paul writing on the injustices associated with withholding wages said, "A just wage is the concrete means of verifying the justice of the whole socioeconomic system."[21] A worker deserves his wages, and it is an injustice to withhold compensation.

Payment for wages must be established primarily because a worker deserves his wages, (Luke 10:7, 1 Tim 5:18), and secondarily because payment for work provides an opportunity to influence the world. In the Old Testament people brought the fruits of their labor as offerings to the Lord, and these fruits sustained the priests in their work (Num 18:8-32, esp v21). Those who reap a reward for their work can share with others in order to support particular causes. Through giving the priests were sustained and the people of God built up. Giving is a way to enable others to perform the dominion they are specifically gifted and called to. It empowers the dominion of others.

Giving is a key component of work that helps further the mission. There are many examples of giving in the bible. The faithful stewarding of goods most likely received from work are seen in those like Barnabas who gave a whole field to the church (Acts 4:36-37), the writings of Luke (Gospel of Luke and Acts) may very well have been enabled because of the giving of a generous sponsor[22] (Luke 1:3). Gaius is another who was likely blessed both monetarily and with a generous spirit, and he opened his home to traveling apostles and an entire church (Rom 16:23)! There are countless examples where faithful labors play a pivotal role in the spread of God's kingdom.

Examples are not in the bible alone. There are many others in our midst today. Some business leaders tithe the profit of their entire business, some give the goods they produce to the needy, and many give regularly to sustain the church. Giving can have a profound effect in furthering God's presence, and we need make sure we grasp this.

An example of this is a friend named Mark who initially grieved going into business and did so only after a failed attempt in ministry. He thought he had sunk to a place of being irrelevant in

---

[21] John Paul II, *Encyclical On Human Work: Laborem Exercens,* (Boston: Daughters of St Paul, 1981), 45.

[22] Darrel L. Bock, *Luke,* Vol. 1, Baker Exegetical Commentary on the New Testament (Grand Rapids: Baker Books, 1994), 63. Bock explains various options for who this person may be.

God's kingdom, but to his surprise he quickly discovered a natural ability at what he called "making deals," and he experienced immediate success. After years in the business world, he summed up his gifting and limitation to me saying, "I'm not gifted as a preacher or teacher. I am gifted in making money." He then began to share how the previous year he completely supported (in addition to giving to his own church and several other causes) two full time missionaries who in turn preached to hundreds of people that year and saw many saved through their work. As he spoke of this, he gave a sly grin and said, "I think I've done what I'm most gifted to do and what most advanced the kingdom."

Mark was right! His gifts and the produce of his work created opportunities to influence many more through his business than he ever would have in full time ministry. He was doing work that mattered, and his gift in business was changing lives for the glory of God.

3.7 Ministering With and As the Church

As we talk about the role of ministry in work, an interlude needs to be taken to see a few connections between the church and our work as ministry. We are not left alone in the mission to change the world. It was God's intent from Eden on that people work with others in the mission. The church is at the heart of God's plan for establishing his kingdom, and we will only be effective in the personal work of ministry when united in corporate ministry.

Martin Luther said, "He who wants to find Christ, must first find the church. How would one know Christ and faith in him if one did not know where they are who believe in him?"[23] The church is a body of believers working together to further the presence of God, and God is making himself known through the church (Eph 3:10). The church is essential to God's mission and to those who want to further his mission.

---

[23] Donald G. Bloesh, *The Church* (Downers Grove: Inter-Varsity Press, 2002), 49.

The church is essential to the mission, because it's essential to the life of a believer. It is the place to hear the word of God preached, enjoy fellowship, pray for others, minister to others, give to God's mission, cultivate spiritual gifts, observe sacraments, and much more. The church is vital, not optional, for those who want to serve the Lord. The church equips believers for the work God has prepared for them, and this often comes from the leaders and teachers in the church (Eph 4:11-12). Pastors and teachers play a significant role in aiding our personal growth and ministry to others.

Though I take great effort to show the opportunity work is for ministry and affirm a priesthood of all believers, this cannot detract from the importance of elders in the church. Not everyone is called to exercise dominion as a pastoral elder, because, like all other work, it has specific qualifications, which includes godly character and the ability to teach and lead (1 Tim 3:1-10, Titus 1). While all Christians are called to work and have an aspect of ministry in their work, not all people are called to lead the church.

The church's goal and our individual goals are the same, and so it needs to be seen that each is to help the other in their common purpose. One way the church helps individual's minister in the marketplace is through the teaching of the word by pastors. Sharing the gospel with others does not always have to come from us and many times it won't, because at times we will struggle with what to say, how to answer certain questions, or simply the right opportunity to say what needs saying. Bringing people to church to hear the word taught is a profound way the ministry of individuals is enhanced by the church.

In doing this the dominion of the church is also spread beyond the church walls to those in the workplace. As Christians venture out to work in the world, they are the church being sent out to care and share the truth with others. They are the church going to unreached places as many of those in the workplace would never set foot in a church building. Workers who find themselves in a difficult job where things seem delightless and chaotic, may in fact be there as the church sent out to bring a transcendent order and peace to their co-workers.

Our personal goal in ministry is the same as the corporate goal of the church, and we are most effective when working together. Since we have the same goal we should work in, with, and through the church to accomplish the priestly calling. William Perkins said in vocation we are "as much as we possibly can, to further the good estate of the church."[24] By furthering the influence of the church we are corporately influencing the world to be what God intends. Those in the marketplace are the church sent out and should be determined to bring others into the church. The church helps them in their mission, and they should find ways to help the church. This connection should lead us to evaluate how the church is helping us and how we are helping it.

3.8 Overcoming Risks

It was mentioned earlier that Adam and Eve's call to work in the garden coupled with the command to have dominion over all the earth implies they were to extend the temple garden to the ends of the earth. They stood on the hillock of this confined garden outside of which lay the expanse of inhospitable land, and "they were to extend the smaller livable area of the garden by transforming the outer chaotic region into a habitable territory."[25] Their expansion would take great sacrifices to leave the comfortable garden area and go outward. They were in the "Garden of Delight" and yet were to go outside of that area to the chaotic, inhospitable, and delightless areas and transform them into the true garden. Such a calling would take a strong desire to overcome complacency and potential risks to accomplish the mission.

People are to have expanding drives that are seeking new territories to influence. It is the reason for new frontiers, missions, innovative technologies, entrepreneurial endeavors, and much more. We should see potential opportunities for gain and glory and desire to go after them. If the effects of cultivating the world are valuable then so is the desire for it.[26] Such desire can reflect a

---

[24] Perkins, 44.

[25] Beal, 82.

[26] R.L. Dabney, *The Practical Philosophy*, (Harrisonburg: Sprinkle, 1984), 81. This is a paraphrase of Dabney.

godly ambition that is the driving force of influencing the uninfluenced.

God's calling should be pursued zealously, but often godly zeal is destroyed when tainted by selfish ambition. Godly zeal should seek God first, being submissive to God and respecting those around us. Selfish ambition is destructive, and its effects are seen every time a business leader is walked to a police car in handcuffs. Selfish ambition is misguided and idolatrous zeal.

The solution to ungodly ambition is not to squash ambition but rather to purify our motives by redirecting them to the right object. This leads to godly ambition. Robert Dabney said, there is a praise worthy ambition that desires to influence and is "uncomplicated by pride, arrogance, calculating selfishness, resentment, hatred of rivals and fear." Such ambition he says is "a virtue" and the "necessary and legitimate energizer of the soul" to great things.[27] This godly ambition can energize a person to seek to overcome great obstacles and take risks in order to influence the world.

Ambition is important, because the greatest opportunities usually require risks. If we never takes risk and never step outside our comfort zone then we will never accomplish anything of significance. Risk should be measured, calculated, and approached with caution (Luke 14:31-33), but never completely rejected. Having a greater influence on the world is a God honoring desire and should be pursued and desired. One should seek to be more influential, to make greater profits, and to be more effective in personal ministry. Seeking such things is good, and we should not be surprised to see these accompanied by risks.

A passion for God and his kingdom should lead to some risk taking. We should take risks to share the word of God. "Don't talk about religion or politics in the office" is the motto of our time, but sharing the word should not be shied away from. We should be wise in what to talk about, where to talk about it, and how to talk about, but by all means do talk about it. At times it may be wiser to build relationships with coworkers at lunch or other times outside the office, but at some point risks have to be taken to share the word.

---

[27] Dabney, 81.

The apostles often caused the greatest uproar when their preaching affected the income of others (Acts 16:36, 19:23-40). Sometimes the word of God will be opposed vigorously. We should not be naïve to think people will always receive it, but that should not keep us from taking risks. We should not be deterred because of "what if's." You might lose a deal, you might offend someone, you may not get the evaluation you like, but you just might change a person's life.

Joe was a sales rep for a company on straight commission and was having a meeting so a client could sign a contract. Their conversation unexpectedly turned to spiritual things, and Joe saw an opportunity. With his income on the line he looked the client straight in the eye and asked, "If you were hit by a truck on your way home and died today would you go to heaven or hell, and why do you believe that?" It startled the client at first, but they began to dialogue, and Joe was able to effectively share the gospel with him. What is amazing about this is that he asked the client the question before the contract was signed! He was willing to risk it all to take advantage of an opportunity to share the gospel.

Such opportunities to influence the world for the glory of God should be sought in order to be more influential in changing the world. Sometimes great business opportunities may need pursuing and sometimes it may be opportunities to share God's word. Risks may involve standing up against some evil, doing something that's right for a customer, taking a particular job, inviting someone to church, sharing the gospel, going to a certain school, or giving in a certain way. Some people may be called to great risks, some may be called to small risks, but one thing is certain, if no risks are taken, then it is likely that very little of lasting significance will ever be accomplished.

3.9 Conclusion

Rob's conversation with the missionary that night had a significant impact on him, and he eventually got it. That night he began a journey of discovering how he could glorify God in his work, and he reordered his life to be missional. Soon he was unashamedly a business man for the glory of God. He grew in his conviction of working with excellence and seeking to serve others with his gifts in business and printing. His work allowed other companies to flourish and grow through his brilliant advertising designs, and with his expertise he helped many companies avoid disastrous decisions. He became a friend to his clients and coworkers, and through his care for them he had many opportunities to pastor people through difficult seasons of life by sharing God's word with them. He also experienced enough financial success to give generously to his church and many others in need. He bought a house that he and his wife graciously opened to many people and would even host weekly church meetings. Rob saw the significant opportunity his work was to influence the world and gain eternal glory, and he took full advantage of it. He is a great example of the powerful effect an ordinary person can have when they understand ministry and work are intended to go hand in hand.

Chapter 3 Discussion Questions

1. How does understanding common grace help you find significance and purpose in your work?

2. What can you do in your current job to extend common grace to others?

3. How can you share the word with others in your work?

4. How are you partnering with the church in the work of ministry?

5. Do you have a godly ambition that is pushing you out into uncomfortable areas?

Chapter 4

Ethics of Work—Dominion in His Image

"So God created man in his own image,
in the image of God he created him;
male and female he created them."
Genesis 1:27

There was a clear difference in the way Alex ran his business—much different than any other person I had been around. Alex was both one of the strongest Christians I knew and one of the most successful businessmen. He had played a pivotal role in the development of major corporations and was now overseeing several of his own successful companies. As I watched him work in his office, I was amazed at his intentionality and determination. He had defined objectives and was making every effort to achieve them. He plowed through to-do lists like a linebacker through a running back. His effectiveness in getting things done was staggering, but there was much more that set his work apart.

Alex also cared deeply about other people, both those that worked for him and those he worked for. His genuine care was evident in the way he enthusiastically greeted people and the patience he showed while discussing complicated business issues. Doing good to others was a main goal of his, and he put a lot of energy into making sure it happened.

In addition to his intentionality and care, Alex was also firmly committed to discipline and accountability in the office. He did not shy away from making or enforcing policies with his employees. He showed a resolute commitment to these and did not back down from the necessary hard decisions. He saw these as crucial for making things better for his company and customers, and yet even these he did with great care and compassion.

Watching Alex work was intriguing to me, because he displayed characteristics that all too often seemed contradictory. I knew business people who were big time go getters, but they usually had little care or concern for others. I also knew business people that were very caring but never got any work done. This balancing of characteristics seemed to make Alex effective, and it seemed to be a way his work was blessing others. People enjoyed working in a caring environment where they got things done, and customers enjoyed knowing they were getting a quality product and top notch service. It seemed everyone enjoyed working for and with Alex. He was clearly doing good to others by both what he did and *how* he did it.

Alex is a great example of *how* we work can glorify God and do good to others. Our work matters to those affected by it. We have a responsibility to work rightly, and when we do our work blesses others. Alex modeled God-glorifying dominion, and what characterized his work are things that characterize God's work. People are created in God image and that means there should be a clear connection between how God works and how we work. Miroslav Volf said, "In the exercise of dominion people function as God's stewards who are responsible to rule over the earth in a way that God rules over his world."[1] One of the great ways we can honor God and serve others is seeking to have what characterizes God's dominion characterize our dominion. By looking to God we learn how to work rightly and also how to balance characteristics that often seem contradictory.

For us to rule as God rules we must know what God's rule is like, and for that reason this chapter examines the attributes of God that people can reflect. Some of God's attributes include holiness, goodness, righteousness, mercy, love, truthfulness, and justice. By looking at who God is we come to understand these characteristics and how we can emulate them. These attributes provide ethical guidelines for God-glorifying work, and they help us see how our work, like God's work, can bless others.

The call to image these characteristics of God also reminds of the privilege and responsibility in work. Only people can reflect

---

[1] Miroslav Volf, *Work in the Spirit: Toward a Theology of Work* (Eugene: Wipf and Stock Publishers, 2001), 47.

these because only they are created in the image of God. Since only people are created in God's image, theologians have said people are "the head and crown of the whole creation."[2] As the crown of creation, people have a unique calling and great responsibility to image the living God. This means our ethical guidelines are never rooted in a list of do's and don'ts but in the very being of God. God himself is our highest ethical standard. Our ethical responsibility is rooted in our incredible privilege, and modeling God's attributes is a way we both glorify him and do good to others, and once again this brings us to doing work that really matters.

4.1 The Attributes of God

The attributes of God listed in this chapter are those that have a particular relevance to work. In the space of this chapter it is only possible to briefly mention some of the various attributes, and then connect them specifically to how people can image them in the work place. These attributes help us understand God, and after understanding how God rules, we are then in a position to know how to image that attribute.

While people are able to reflect who God is, it is important to know they will never reflect him perfectly. People are not God, they are his image, and a fallen image at that, so they are not capable of doing exactly what God does. There are obvious limitations to the extent we can image God, but that should not hinder us from looking to him and discovering how to work in the world for his glory. The goal of learning about these attributes is not that we are able to reflect them perfectly, but that we better know who God is and what he calls us to do. We will now look at God's attributes of dominion, authority, goodness, justice and righteousness, truthfulness, holiness, and creativity.

---

[2] Herman Bavinck, *Reformed Dogmatics,* vol 2 (Grand Rapids: Baker, 2004), 531.

4.2 Dominion

Dominion has been discussed in previous chapters but is mentioned again in order to clearly connect the other attributes to it. God reigns supreme over all things and is in the process of bringing all things under his reign. His dominion is his governing of all things, and more specifically the "continued activity where He rules all things (with the end in mind) so as to secure the accomplishment of His divine purpose."[3] God has a purpose in mind for all he does, and he is in the process of bringing all things together to accomplish his purposes.

God rules over all things in every way. He gives life and breath to all people (Acts 17:25) and sustains the universe by his powerful word (Heb 1:3). His dominion is far reaching sustaining the life of a single sparrow and the hairs on a person's head (Matt 10:29-31). He guides the decisions of rulers (Prov 21:1) and even brings one nation against another (Amos 6:14). He promotes some people and brings others down (Psalm 75:6-7). Even the haphazard events of life are governed by him (Proverbs 16:33).

God does not let things happen in life for no reason, nor are they beyond his control. Proverbs 16:4 says "The Lord works out everything for his own ends," so as God governs all things he is ultimately working all things together for specific purposes. He is fully in control at all times and is governing all things in order to bring about his intended goals.

While no person could ever reign exactly how God reigns, we are able to reflect his dominion in some ways. People reflect God's governance in the orchestration of what is put under them for the achieving of a purpose. A manager looks at his objectives for the week to determine what needs to be done and then brings those objectives to completion. It is good and right to have objectives and to seek to accomplish them. People reflect God's dominion as they work to achieve purposes and bring about results in the world, and the goal of their governing should ultimately be in line with God's goal.

---

[3] Louis Berkhoff, *Systematic Theology*, (Grand Rapids: Eerdmans, 1996), 175.

Perhaps the most important reason to mention God's dominion is because it can be a great source of encouragement to us. No person is omnipotent and able to control all things, so when things go unexpectedly, when they take a turn for the worse, or when a situation cannot be changed that is when we trust and worship the one who is in ultimate control. We trust his governance and that he is working all things, even the things beyond our control, for our good and his glory. As we grow in understanding God's other attributes, it will become even easier for us to trust his dominion.

4.3 Authority

Since God exercises dominion over all things and is creator of all things, he has the right to have authority over all creation. This is a distinctive part of his Lordship. God is supreme over all, and as Lord of all, he is the one to whom all things must obey. All things must give an account to him, and he demonstrates his authority by commanding how all should serve him. James 4:12 says, "There is only one Lawgiver and Judge, the one who is able to save and destroy." His giving of law is a primary way his authority is exercised and enforced.

As the lawgiver he is ultimately the one to whom all must answer and give an account to. Stephen Charnock said, "Commanding always supposes an authority in the person giving the precept; it obligates the person to whom the command is directed."[4] God gives his law to his people and through this law he demonstrates his authority over them, and they demonstrate their allegiance to him through obedience. God commands how people are to honor him, and he holds people accountable through his law.

It is important to note that a main reason God gives commands is to bless others. Deuteronomy 4:5-6 demonstrates this as Moses speaks to the people saying,

---

[4] Stephen Charnock, *The Existence and Attributes of God* (Minneapolis: Klock&Klock Christian Publishers, 1969), 685.

> See, I have taught you decrees and laws as the LORD my God commanded me, so that you may follow them in the land you are entering to take possession of it. Observe them carefully, for this will show your wisdom and understanding to the nations, who will hear about all these decrees and say, "Surely this great nation is a wise and understanding people."

These verses show God's commands are for the good of others, teaching them how to live and function in the world. God's word lights our path showing what should and should not be done. Through his law people see murder, lying, and stealing are bad, and they know how to do good to others by extending kindness, truthfulness, and generosity. His commands are for the good of his people and function to help them know how to live rightly in the world he has created. This should lead those under his authority to give thanks for his commands.

Through dominion God also gives people the ability to have authority and rule over others, and this authority is often expressed through their giving and enforcing of commands, rules, and laws. The exercise of such authority images God and should also be done for the good of others. This is likely why the Bible commands authorities to be supported (Rom 13:1). The establishing and enforcing of authority should ultimately have the good of others in mind (Rom 13:4), so whether it is a person working for Homeland Security setting policies that allow the nation's infrastructure to be monitored and protected from terrorist attacks, or a small business owner deciding who works on what days, both offer opportunities to emulate and glorify God by establishing laws that do good to others.

Those who are in authority must also recognize they too are under authority, and their authority should honor the commands of the one they serve. They will be held accountable to God's standards for ruling, so they should issue laws that are good. Their laws or policies dictate and describe how work is to be done and conducted. This takes away ambiguity and should instill good, clear, and beneficial procedures. These policies are to be good, not overbearing, and they should be for the betterment of others.

Exercising authority is part of extending dominion, and it is a way God's goodness and care can be demonstrated to the world. People should be grateful God spells out the dangers of lying, killing, stealing, or the folly of laziness. They should also be appreciative of procedures set at workplaces, such as those detailing how parents can safely checkout their newborn babies from the hospital, or those of the human resource department that require different forms for different doctor in order to ensure accurate billing. These rules are established and enforced for the good of others.

We should also note here that God alone knows all things from the beginning to the end, and he alone is able to give perfect laws. People are not all-knowing and therefore often make policies that will need to be updated, changed, or abolished. It is not always wrong to desire to change policies, but this process should be done in a way that indicates respect for the One in ultimate authority. Even our opposition to unjust laws should be done in a way that glorifies God and is consistent with his other attributes. The desire to see rules or policies changed can be a godly desire that seeks to improve the business, product, or quality of life, and as a noble desire it should be pursued diligently and in a way that observes God's authority.

4.4 Goodness

It is a fearful thing to see an evil dictator come to power. They rule with an iron fist, and though the reign of their dominion extends far and wide, they do no good for their people. God's dominion and authority are extremely encouraging to us, because God is good. He is good, and he models a goodness that people should emulate. His goodness is well defined by A.W. Tozer,

> The goodness of God is that which disposes him to be kind, cordial, benevolent, and full of good will toward men. He is tenderhearted and of quick sympathy, and his unfailing attitude toward all moral beings is open, frank, and

friendly. By his nature he is inclined to bestow blessedness, and he takes holy pleasure in the happiness of his people.[5]

Tozer later goes on to say, "That God is good is taught or implied on every page of the Bible and must be received as an article of faith as impregnable as the throne of God."[6] Few can state better than Tozer what the goodness of God consists of and how pervasive a theme it is. His goodness involves his love, mercy, and faithfulness to others, and it is his attribute of goodness that makes his dominion and authority so very comforting. As God rules and reigns over the universe, he is doing good.

James 1:17 says, "Every good and perfect gift is from above," reminding us every good thing we receive comes from the hand of God. He is the source of all good and is to be thanked for it. His goodness extends to all people as "he causes his sun to rise on the evil and the good, and sends rain on the righteous and the unrighteous" (Matt 5:45). God extends his goodness to everyone, both to those who love and honor him and even those who hate him. He is good to all people providing rain for their crops and food for their needs. All good comes from God and all people experience his goodness in many ways. No person will ever be able to say God was not good to them.

We will express the goodness of God when we first acknowledge and appreciates his goodness too us. We should recognize all his provision and thank him for it. The psalmist saw God's goodness and rejoiced in it saying, "Praise the LORD. Give thanks to the LORD, for he is good" (Psalm 106:1). Many fail to show goodness in their dominion, because they fail to see God's goodness to them. It is a gift from God that you have the ability to work, that your employer hired you, or that you work with people you like (or even mostly like), and things like these should be celebrated. We live in an imperfect world, and there will be aspects of work that are not perfect, but even in imperfect situations God's goodness is present. Recognizing his goodness will better prepare us to extend goodness to others. Many distraught and downcast

---

[5] A.W. Tozer, *Knowledge of the Holy* (San Francisco: Harper Collins, 1961), 82.

[6] Ibid.

souls could be encouraged by remembering they are under the care of a good Lord, and his goodness is always present. This brings contentment and peace so that our work is done with joy rather than anxiety.

God is good to those under his care, and our dominion is an opportunity to extend good to others. Galatians 6:10 says, "Therefore, as we have opportunity, let us do good to all people." Extending goodness could come in the form of a kind word instead of a spiteful comment or it could come by doing what's best for the customer rather than what most lines our pockets.

There will be times in work where hard decisions and difficult actions need to be made, but goodness should still characterize these actions. There will be times where an employee, even a good employee will need to be let go. The goodness of God demands these difficult decisions be made with respect and goodwill toward the person. Even when the employee is one you are glad to be rid of, rather than being excited to punish the person (and possibly wound him for how he wounded you), God's goodness to the unrighteous demands we seek to do that person good even in their termination. The goodness we show to others does not flow from the good they have done to us, but rather from the goodness God has shown to us. We are to reflect God's goodness and not the goodness (or lack of goodness) of others.

There will indeed be times where justice needs to be served in the work place. Justice is an attribute of God and should be expressed, but justice is done with good in mind. It is done to serve the person, teach right from wrong, and ultimately better that person and the organization. Just as God's dominion is characterized by an intent to bless and take pleasure in the happiness of others so too should our dominion be characterized by the same. It is an expression of loving others as God has loved us.

4.5 Justice and Righteousness

These two attributes could be dealt with independently, but because of their tight connection I deal with them together. God's justice implies he judges, and for his judgments to be just he must have a righteous standard to judge by. God is righteous and the overflow of his righteousness is that justice is established. These two attributes always imply the other.

"God's righteousness means that God always acts in accordance with what is right and is himself the final standard of what is right."[7] This gets at the meaning of the word "righteous" in the Bible, which often means one is right in a moral sense. It means things are as they are supposed to be, and in relation to law righteousness means one is correctly aligned with the law. The word is often used in courtroom settings to indicate a person is without fault and free from guilt.

To apply this to God means that if God were brought to court no one could find anything against him. All his ways are right and just. He is wholly good and without evil. God never contradicts the laws he has established. This is seen in Matthew 5:48 "Be perfect, therefore, as your heavenly Father is perfect," and Psalm 119:137 "Righteous are you, O LORD, and your laws are right." God does no wrong in his ruling over the world.

God is righteous doing no wrong, so all his verdicts and decisions are just and right. He renders to every man as he deserves without partiality, favor, or blindness.[8] God gives to each as they merit and shows no favoritism or neglect. He does not condemn the innocent, pardon the guilty, punish with undue severity, nor pass over what should be punished. He judges with complete righteousness (Psalm 96:13) and is just in all his ways (Deut 32:4).

In righteousness God judges the world according to his laws, and his judgments involve both punishment and reward. Louis Berkhofff said in regards to God judging, "He has instituted a moral government in the world, and imposed a just law upon man, with promises of reward for the obedient and threats of punishment for the (disobedient)."[9] God judges people according to what they have done (Matt 25:21, 34), and people also imitate this. Bosses determine what employees are worth and what type of

---

[7] Wayne Grudem, *Systematic Theology* (Grand Rapids: Zondervan, 1994), 203.

[8] Charles Hodge, *Systematic Theology,* vol 1 (Grand Rapids:Eerdmans, 1995), 416. Paraphrase.

[9] Berkof, 75.

reward or compensation they should receive. The paying of a salary requires judgment and is an example of imitating God. God also brings punishment to those who deserve it (Rom 2:9, 2 Thes 1:8), and people image this as well. When a person acts unrighteously it is just to punish them, and depending on the severity of the offense the penalty may be more or less severe. A person who steals from the company may be terminated for the offense, whereas a person who is late may receive a verbal warning. The various offenses require consequences that correspond appropriately.

God has given all people the ability to make decisions, but some jobs are focused mainly on providing judgments. A judge on the Supreme Court decides policy for a nation, counselors hear differences between husbands and wives, and office managers evaluate employee performances. By nature certain positions focus on making judgments on others, and when we find ourselves in such roles we must make decisions that are just and right.

When the person making judgments is not righteous injustice will prevail. This happens when a boss decides to promote his friend as opposed to a more qualified person of a different race or sex, or when a coach overlooks players using steroids, because it improves his chances of winning. To be just requires a righteous character that desires to see justice experienced by all.

On judgment day God will judge the entire world with justice and an exacting standard. There will be no favoritism, partiality, or escaping his justice. That day brings accountability to the way we execute and enforce justice, because our judgment and standards will come under his judgment and standards. We must live according to God's standard of right and wrong, and not according to our own standard.

Psalm 19:8 says the righteousness of God's precepts brings joy to the heart. Just as God's righteous precepts bring joy to our heart, we will have much joy when righteousness is present on earth. People often dislike their work because of the wickedness and evil they see. One of the great joys of heaven will be that nothing unrighteous or evil is allowed in. Contemplating this future world of complete righteousness will bring joy to our heart, and so will seeing glimmers of righteousness and justice established on earth now.

4.6 Truthfulness

When most see this heading, the verse, "Thou shall not lie" probably rolls off the tongue. That is a great verse to know, and one that people all too quickly forget about in business today, but God's truthfulness is more than simply not lying. It has been said that "God's truthfulness is displayed as faithfulness in what he plainly promises."[10] God does what he says he will do, and when he makes a promise, he does it plainly and without ambiguity. His truthfulness is seen in that he is not able to lie (Heb 6:18), deceive, or change his mind (Numbers 23:19). His truthfulness means he is ethically reliable. If God were not truthful he would not be worthy of trust or faith.

Scripture clearly teaches that people should be truthful as well. It means we speak clearly and plainly without ambiguity (2 Cor 4:2). Some people avoid plain talk to prevent others from being able to hold them liable, which is just as wrong as lying. Lawyers can earn big money talking around questions, and business people can make deals by speaking evasively. In doing so they manipulate others and fail to glorify God.

Truthfulness also means that we are faithful to what we say or commit to. We do not say one thing one moment and something different another moment. The apostle Paul exemplified this saying, "When I planned this, did I do it lightly? Or do I make my plans in a worldly manner so that in the same breath I say, 'Yes, yes' and 'No, no?'" (2 Corinthians 1:17). Our words should have weight, because our character and integrity are attached to our faithfulness to do what we say. If we say something and do not do it we have lied. This is the reason a righteous man "keeps his oath even when it hurts." (Psalm 15:4). Such commitment to our speech stands in stark contrast to our culture, but it rightly applies God's standard of truth.

---

[10] Heinrich Heppe, *Reformed Dogmatics,* trans G.T. Thompson, Editor Ernst Bizer (Grand Rapids: Baker Book House, 1950), 98.

One last point on truth is to see its relation to what something is. Charles Hodge said, "The primary idea of truth is that which sustains, which does not fail, or disappoint our expectations."[11] The true is the real. In saying this Hodge talks of God as the true God (John 17:3) as opposed to the many false god's who have no dominion, who are not holy, who have no power, and who are by nature nothing. God demonstrates himself as the true God again and again. He is the real God opposed to the imaginary or false gods. For us, this demands not only truthfulness in what we say but honesty in what we make ourselves appear to be. Appearing to be something we are not is untruthful and follows the example of Satan who masquerades as an angel of light (2 Cor 11:14). When people make their business appear more stable and secure than it is or customers misrepresent their situation in hopes of "getting a great deal" they are being untruthful. Actions like this hurt others. It is imperative that people accurately represent who they are and what their intentions are. God in his justice will one day make all things known and show such people for what they truly are. No one should pretend to be what they are not, because one day God will reveal the truth.

4.7 Holiness

Holiness is a term we may be somewhat familiar with by its association with religious terms like holy priest, holy book, or Holy Grail, but the concept behind this word often eludes us. Holiness is taught many places in the bible and is used many times to describe God and men. In reference to God, Don Bloesh said, "God's holiness is his majestic purity that cannot tolerate moral evil."[12]

Holiness implies an absolute moral perfection and a complete freedom from the presence of evil. It demands moral purity and abhorrence for sin. God's holiness is seen in that his eyes are too pure to look on evil, and he does not tolerate wrong

---

[11] Hodge, 436.
[12] Donald Bloesch, *God Almighty* (Downers Grove: InterVarsity Press, 1995), 140.

(Hab 1:13). He is completely free from evil and any moral imperfections,[13] and because he alone is holy he alone is the one all people will worship (Rev 15:4). God's holiness shows he is completely free from any evil and completely devoted to what is good. He is absolutely perfect in all his being and attributes, neither doing nor tolerating any wrong.

The holiness of God is what makes the unholy or less holy tremble with fear when they are in his presence. This is the testimony of the prophet Isaiah when he had a vision of God and saw the Lord seated on His throne high and exalted (Isaiah 6:1). In this vision heavenly creatures were worshipping God saying "Holy, holy, holy is the Lord Almighty; the whole earth is full of his glory." Their voices shook the doors and the temple was filled with smoke. At this encounter with God Isaiah cried, "Woe to me! I am ruined! For I am a man of unclean lips and live among a people of unclean lips, and my eyes have seen the King, the Lord Almighty" (Isaiah 6:5). The presence of the holy led Isaiah to recognize his utter depravity and unholiness.

No person is completely free of evil like God, and all would be undone like Isaiah in the presence of God. When holy is used to describe other objects, people, or places it is not used in an absolute sense but rather to denote something that is being set apart for a special purpose, a purpose dedicated to God. This is seen in holy ground (Exd 3:5), holy assembly (Exod 12:16), holy city (Neh 11:1), and countless other examples. It indicates these things are "set apart from general use and placed in a special relation to God and his service."[14] Things become holy not because of a change in their substance, but because of their dedication to serving the one who is truly holy.

When God commands people to "Be holy as I am holy" (Lev 19:2, 1 Pet 1:15-16) he is not saying, "Be as holy as I am." That would be impossible. Rather these verses call one to remove itself from the "character it has in common with all other things and to impress upon it another stamp."[15] It is to be characterized by devotion to the thing it is set apart for, so when God calls people to

---

[13] Hodge, 413.

[14] Bavinck, 217.

[15] Ibid, 219. This is paraphrase of Bavinck.

be holy he calls them to be devoted to him, and that devotion is to give them a distinct character. Their character is no longer of the world or the people around them. It is a character defined by disdain for evil and commitment to moral purity.

Christians are to be holy in all that they do. They are to have a higher ethic. Speech is to be holy, thoughts are to be holy, and contracts are to be holy. For our dominion to be holy everything in it must be holy. It is to be pure and free of evil, as set apart for a holy purpose. All things are to be done without evil or impurity of any kind.

While no person will ever be holy like God, Christians should have recognition of a higher calling in their work and therefore a purer ethic. The standard for how we live and work is not that of other people, but rather God himself. The person who slanders a competitor because that competitor slandered them has lost the true standard for their work. We must look vertically to God who is our standard and not horizontally to those around us.

As soon as holiness becomes a criteria or command for work all of our goals must be qualified. It is no longer commendable to have success without holiness. Those who say "It's nothing personal it's just business," are typically living wholly for themselves in an unholy manner, and their thoughtless cliché fails to justify the horrendous acts that usually follow. It is utterly absurd for a person to assume to be committed to serving the holy God and have no concern for the manner they accomplish their work. Holiness demands a person see their work as set apart for a different purpose. They are to image and honor the one who is truly holy and tolerates no wrong.

4.8 Creativity

Read the account of creation in Genesis 1 or God's many works in nature that the psalmist celebrates in Psalm 104, and you are confronted with the creativity of God. These passages show God as the source of all animals, plants, fish, land, sky, water, everything in creation, and the one who designed them to work together. It is an amazing picture of the wisdom and creativity of God that brings such beautiful diversity to the world.

God could have made everything the same. Animals could have all been the same size, shape and color, and the surface of the earth could have had the same foliage, topography, and climate, but he did not do that. God's creativity is on display in creation, and it declares his glory (Psalm 19:1). Living in Orlando, FL for several years spoiled me because of the opportunity to see the creativity of God. Nearby parks housed massive killer whales from the Arctic, oddly shaped octopuses from the warm waters of Australia, fluorescent plankton from the depths of ocean bottoms, and tiny sea horses whose ornate bodies seemed to defy practicality. All these had unique purposes in the underwater world they lived in, and while God could have created everything alike he didn't do that. He made them different, and all contribute to his purposes in their own unique way.

While most theologians do not consider creativity an essential attribute of God, I include it, because it describes God, is important to work, and uniquely brings together several attributes already mentioned. Creativity is important to life. Artists, musicians, and actors creatively work and perform in ways that enhance life with entertainment and enjoyment. But creativity is also necessary in many other professions. Problems are constantly posed in offices that require creative rather than bland solutions. Electrical engineers need creativity to discover solutions that push the limits of resolution and quality for televisions. Physical therapists need creative ways to motivate their patients through painful rehab in order to maximize the recovery. God enhances life through his grand creativity and people should too.

It also needs to be said that while God demonstrates great creativity, he does so without contradicting or abandoning his other attributes like goodness, righteousness, and holiness. This is important, because most people today associate being creative with stepping out of the bounds of goodness and holiness. Hollywood makes a living mass producing low quality films that are simply a rehash of an old plot and "creatively" redone with a scandalous sex scene or graphic violence. It is easy to use vile creativity to attract a crowd, but these production are not good nor are they holy and God-honoring. Creativity should be done in line with the other attributes, because they are what make truly creative work so good. We must not abandon creativity because of the way the world abuses it. We must redeem it for the glory of God. Creative work accompanied with goodness, holiness, and righteousness will bring quality work that is also God glorifying.

4.9 Direction and Hope for the Image of God

The attributes of God paint a multifaceted picture of what it looks like to rule as God rules and bless people through work. They bring definition to God-glorifying dominion and the high calling his image bearers have. The complexity of the attributes shows us our incredible responsibility, which in turn points us to God's word and the gospel.

Imaging God's attributes is no doubt a difficult and great responsibility. Each of these attributes is part of who God is, and if one part were taken away God would not be God. What would God be without his dominion? What would he be if he were not righteous? In a similar way all of God's attributes effect one another. God's governing is fully affected in every way by his holiness, by his goodness, by his justice. Likewise, without dominion God's goodness, holiness, and justice might lack expression and lie in obscurity.[16] We see God's goodness through his dominion over the world and his dominion gives greater expression to his goodness.

All of God's attributes are fully present in all he does, and they should be present in his people too. Our dominion is an opportunity to reflect God to the world and bring expression to what God calls us to be and do, and all the other attributes are to be fully present in what we do. We are not to forsake holiness for the sake of dominion nor goodness for the sake of justice. We cannot exercise God-like dominion without all the attributes being present.

There is much more that we could discuss to better understand how to rule like God: we could say much more about

---

[16] Charnock, 666. Says "Without this dominion some perfections, such as justice and mercy would lie in obscurity, and much of his wisdom would be shrouded from our sight and knowledge."

each of these attributes, talk about them in specific situations, or even talk about the many other attributes of God like his knowledge, power, patience, grace, mercy, and sovereignty. But rather than talk about these, it is better to talk about where we can gain direction on how to image God in the many various situations of life. To do this we turn to the word of God. The word of God gives direction on how we can rightly live in the world, and at the center of God's word is the expectation to imitate God in his character and conduct. God himself is our moral standard, and this is what his word points to. John Frame says,

> (God's) moral standard is simply himself, his person, his nature… for the most part, his law instructs us to imitate his character and conduct. He made us in his image to be like him… so the righteousness that God expects from us is essentially to image his own ethical character—his love, his holiness, his righteousness… what he commands of us is what he himself is and does.[17]

The character of God is what we should image, and it is what his word leads to when properly followed. God himself is the very essence of what we seek to emulate when we obey his word. As Calvin says, "God has so depicted his character in the law that if any man carries out in deeds whatever is enjoined there, he will express the image of God, as it were in his own life."[18] Learning who God is in his word leads us to both trust him and know how to honor him in the many different situations we find ourselves in.

It is a high calling to rule as God rules, and as we grow in understanding God's word we will inevitable see how frequently we fail to rule like God. Who can say they have been truthful in all their actions, or just in all their ways, or holy, or good. No one has completely lived up to God's standard. Man was created in the image of God, but our sin has corrupted and distorted that image. Our sinful actions make standing before a holy God a fearful thing. But there is good news for those whose sin has vandalized God's

---

[17] John Frame, *Doctrine of God* (Phillipsburg: P&R Publishing, 2002), 448-9.

[18] John Calvin, *Institutes,* 2.8.51.

image, and it is in this good news that God's glorious attributes culminate. God's justice and righteousness demanded sin be punished, and yet God did not give up on doing good to his creation. In his infinite wisdom and creativity God designed a way to punish sin, save sinners, and receive all the glory for it. He did it by sending his son Jesus Christ, who is his exact image, to live a perfect life and atone for the sins of his people by dying on the cross. In doing so God proved truthful to all his promises in the past, upheld his justice with complete righteousness, exerted his dominion by triumphing over all other powers, and did it all in perfect holiness.

Through Jesus Christ sinners can be reconciled to a holy God and renewed in the image of the creator (Colossians 3:10). Through the renewal that comes from being in Christ, people are enabled to live properly toward God, toward neighbors and toward the world.[19] The penalty and power of sin has been broken, and there is hope of forgiveness for failures and also for becoming more like him. The gospel enables us to grow in expressing God's image and instills hope that one day we will be without blemish in a renewed world. It helps us see more fully how the attributes of God's authority, mercy, justice, creativity, holiness, dominion, and goodness are all brought together in the most amazingly perfect way, and it inspires us to worship, serve, trust, and emulate God.

God's multifaceted character provides the basis for how we are to rule in the world and brings definition to our dominion. In it we see a profound way we can bless others and do work that really matters. If we are going to glorify God we must rule as he himself rules, and that means the things that characterize him should characterize us. His word gives direction on how we can imitate him and his gospel gives hope for forgiveness and change. It is in the character of God we find our ethical standards and discover how to hold together attributes that often seem contradictory, and it is all to the glory of God.

---

[19] Anthony Hoekema, *Created in God's Image* (Grand Rapids: Eerdmans, 1994), 86. This sentence is a slight adaptation from the main ways Hoekema shows the image is renewed toward God, neighbor and nature.

Conclusion

One last great example of a person working with a Godward focus and blessing others through the way they work occurs in the book of Ruth. Ruth and her mother in law Naomi are widows who return home to Israel after the death of their husbands. Ruth is a Moabite who faithfully stays by Naomi's side, because she wants to serve the Lord. With no husband to protect them, no family to return to, and no means of making a living these women were extremely vulnerable. Their only means of survival is for Ruth to roam in grain fields behind the hired workers picking up scraps.

Ruth is working in the fields when Boaz arrives on the scene. Boaz is known as worthy man. He is noble and valiant. He passes his reapers and utters his first words, "The Lord be with you!" (Ruth 2:4). When he sees Ruth he extends kindness to this helpless foreign widow. He tells her to glean in his field, to take a drink from his worker's water when she is thirsty, and he instructs the men not to touch her. Additionally, he also tells his men to leave some sheaves for her and even pull out some of what they harvested to leave behind for her.

The story unfolds and Boaz decides to marry Ruth and redeem her, but he knows God's word and that according to it the first right to redeem Ruth falls to another relative. Boaz doesn't worry, fret, or even attempt to lie as many others would. He trusts God and speaks directly, openly, and truthfully to the other man about the situation. The man declines to marry Ruth, and Boaz immediately acts (with ten other men present as witnesses) to confirm his intention to marry Ruth.

Throughout the story Boaz is a man of noble character (as is Ruth) demonstrating great faithfulness both to God and others. Boaz honors the Lord and that leads him to extending dominion that blesses others. He demonstrates righteousness, goodness, truthfulness, mercy, and much more, and in the book there is a common refrain of people speaking a blessing to Boaz for what he has done (Ruth 2:4, 2:20, 4:11). His work and life have a powerful effect on others. He serves a God who is good, righteous, just, merciful, faithful, and truthful, and he demonstrates those same characteristics in all that he does, and others are blessed by his dominion over them. His work makes a difference to others, and he is another compelling example that how we work really does matter.

Chapter 4 Discussion Questions

1. How does connecting God's attributes with your calling to image him help you see your ethical responsibility in your work? How does it help you see that *how* you work can bless other people?

2. What attribute seems most challenging for you to embody in your work? What attributes seem most difficult to balance and not let go of one for the sake of the other?

3. What attribute of God is most encouraging to you as your work under his dominion.

Chapter 5

Blood, Sweat, and Thistles—Working Under the Curse

"Cursed is the ground because of you;
through painful toil you will eat of it all the days of your life."
Genesis 3:17

It was a warm Saturday morning, and my wife and I were just finishing a big pancake breakfast in our newly acquired first home. We bought the house as a fixer-upper in 2004, thinking with the real estate wave on the rise it would a great way to make some money while in graduate school. We were into our third month of being there, and the house still needed many repairs. The current project was the sprinkler system, which had become my nemesis. After replacing virtually the entire system, one unexpected part after another, I had become fairly adept at repairing it and was ready for battle. I stood up after our delightful breakfast, kissed my beautiful wife, and confidently told her I would be back in about twenty to thirty minutes as the current problem was "an easy fix."

Hours later I was still working on it. My first attempt actually went great. That is until I turned on the sprinkler system and realized that in the process of fixing the broken pipe my saw had nicked the large main pipe below it. Now, while the first pipe was fixed, a bigger pipe was gushing water about ten feet high. I then had to cut through the pipe I just fixed in order to repair the one below. A couple trips to the store for parts I didn't have (and didn't think I would need) proved quite a test.

After another repair, I thought it was finally fixed and turned on the sprinkler system again to see if my work was a success. It worked. That is for about ten seconds, and then the fitting slipped, because apparently the glue didn't set. This wouldn't be that big of a deal except this time I was fairly certain that a pool of water around the broken section had risen high enough that it would get sucked into the pipe along with large amounts of sand, creating an even bigger problem. At this point I had enough of my "easy fix." I turned the system off, threw my shovel down, and proceeded to tell the sprinkler system what I really thought about it.

In this moment, it was not just the sprinkler system that was getting to me. It was everything. The fence I thought would take a week to put up took three months, the amount I thought it would cost to paint the house tripled, and the old roof I hoped would last a few more years was ruined by the first hurricane in thirty years. I sat down on the ground and with my face on my hands uttered with exasperation, "Why does it have to be so hard?"

If you have ever uttered (or wanted to utter) this statement, then this chapter is for you. This chapter isn't in college textbooks, it certainly won't make it into the self-help section of the local book store, and it probably won't appear on many short lists of reads about becoming a better worker, yet it could be one of the most valuable lessons about work. If we can't answer why things are so hard or only have superficial answers we are doomed to labor in constant frustration and may never give the consistent effort required for doing anything that really matters.

5.1 A Fallen World

The reason work is so hard is because the world is fallen. People rebelled against God's perfect will, and the judgment for their sin was a curse. This curse did not create work but rather made work difficult. John Murray said, "It should be noted that the curse is not the curse of labor; the curse is the pain and hardship connected with labor."[1] In attempting to show the value and significance of work we must not construct an idealized understanding of work that ignores its difficulties. If we are going to honor God and work for his glory then we must be prepared to encounter the difficulty that the curse brings, and for this reason we examine the effects of the fall. Genesis 3:17-19 says,

---

[1] John Murray, *Principles of Conduct,* 82.

> Cursed is the ground because of you; through painful toil you will eat of it all the days of your life. It will produce thorns and thistles for you, and you will eat the plants of the field. By the sweat of your brow you will eat your food until you return to the ground, since from it you were taken; for dust you are and to dust you will return.

The ground is cursed here, and as ground is symbolic for all toil done under the sun, the curse makes all work for all people difficult.

Work takes on distinctively new characteristics after the fall. We will look at the specific changes mentioned in the verse, but it is important to first talk about the broader consequences of the fall and show how these consequences also contribute to the difficulty of work. The fall brought drastic changes to the entire world. It brought death so that people are destined to die: no one will live forever (Gen 3:19). It brought a corruption of human nature, so that all people from Adam forward inherit a sinful nature and are no longer able not to sin. Their inclinations are evil (Gen 6:5), and they sin in thoughts, words, and actions. These evil intentions carry over to even the most intimate of relationships, so there is enmity even between husbands and wives (Gen 3:16). Spouses compete against rather than complement one another, and this competition bleeds into other relationships. There is an ongoing battle between the forces of good and evil, between the seed of the woman and the seed of the serpent (Gen 3:15). And finally, because of the fall people are expelled from the presence of God in the Garden (Gen 3:23). They abandoned God, and now God banishes them from the Garden "like a landlord expelling unsatisfactory tenants."[2]

These broad effects have a direct bearing on the difficulty we encounter in work. Human corruption affects it, because people are sinners. They lie, cheat, and steal. The realm of evil affects work because it urges and feeds people's desire to sin. Enmity affects marriages and also business relationships, so that people

---

[2] T.D. Alexander, *From Paradise to Promise Land* (Grand Rapids: Baker Academic, 2002), 132.

compete against rather than complement others in the office. A lack of direct access to God leaves people wondering about decisions and searching for answers to problems.

These effects of the fall explain the difficult environment that we live in. It clarifies why things are the way they are: why people sin, why there is evil, why things are hard, why we don't hear from God directly. A biblical understanding helps make sense of the difficulties in the office and also at home. All of life is affected by the fall. If we think only work is affected by the fall we will be tempted to flee from it only to encounter the curse in other areas—like marriage, children, friendships, and even dream vacations. We live in a fallen world and will experience its consequences in every part of life.

5.2 The Difficulty of Work

In Genesis 3:17 God curses the ground, which is the object of work. The word "curse" that appears in Genesis 3 can seem a bit foreign to most of us today. When we think of a curse it usually involves an adventure movie about pirates whose experiences of a curse seem far removed from our lives. When used in the Bible "curse" usually means to ensnare with obstacles. It involves hemming in or binding a person. It is essentially to render someone ineffective in what they do.[3] This means the curse on the ground hinders people from achieving the very purposes they were created.

We saw in Genesis 1 that prior to the fall, the word dominion implied subduing something that did not wish to be subdued. The task of subduing was never without difficulty, but now there is a heightening resistance to it. Under the curse work takes on a qualitative change and has an increased resistance to the hands of people. T.D. Alexander explains this change saying,

> No longer is the ground divinely empowered to produce food in abundance. Man must work by the sweat of his brow in order to eat. Furthermore, his task is made more

---

[3] Harris, *Theological Wordbook of the Old Testament*, 168.

88

difficult because the ground will produce thorns and thistles. No longer is the man at harmony with the ground from which he was taken and upon which he depends for food.[4]

In the Garden of Eden before the fall work certainly required an expenditure of energy, but that effort was largely characterized by peace, harmony, and security, and these are largely what are missing from the world after the fall. Work is now hard. Nothing else should be expected when we work.

In the curse we are told several things that depict the difficulty in work. The first is that it is now through "painful toil" that people will eat. Work is not easy, and the land gives its produce reluctantly, only after much coercion. The word for pain here is the same word used in Genesis 3:16 to talk about the increase of pain in the woman's labor at childbirth. The pain of a woman in labor is intense. The process is physically exhausting, and the birth of the child takes every bit of strength in body and mind. There is a similar implication for work. Though the pain is not as concentrated as in birth, it is felt deeply.

I was recently talking to a friend who was in the midst of a significant writing project, and I asked him how it was going. He shared the great consternation of bringing his thoughts on months of research into a concise and understandable manner. After sharing the great difficulties he was encountering, he said, "I feel like I am trying to give birth." Now I would never say those exact words (especially not in hearing distance of my wife), but there is some truth to what he said. Bringing forth a cultivated and beneficial product that is profitable to others comes at great labor, and labor that is often painfully hard. There will be times where we are hurt, exasperated, or exhausted—almost as if giving birth.

The curse also causes sweat in work. Pain reminds that work will hurt. Sweat reminds that great effort is required. Sweat is the product of exertion and indicates there will be much that has to be overcome. This exertion will be felt in every farmer struggling to carry the last bale of hay to the barn or the banker struggling to

---

[4] Alexander, 132.

account for that last dollar. Things never just fall into place but instead come through intense effort.

Knowing great effort is required for work should keep us pushing on when things get hard. My father-in-law is a contractor and has unintentionally passed on a saying to me that he usually utters when things go wrong. Like when you are standing on scaffolding to the second story straining to put in a heavy window and you realize the window is too big for the frame or when you're digging a new water line and realize the ground you have to cut through is solid rock. After a deep sigh, he usually utters matter-of-factly, "It's never easy." Things never go the way we want or would like. It is always much harder. By acknowledging the difficulty he essentially acknowledges the need for more effort and resolve, and we should do the same when things get hard.

Another difficulty of the curse is thorns and thistles. Thorns and thistles are pesky plants that pop up out of nowhere and grow at a staggering rate (certainly faster than the things you are working so diligently to cultivate). They are little things that can cause big problems. Thorns and thistle grow in the very place that good crops grow, and they must be constantly tended or they will choke out the good plants. If not tended to they can destroy an entire harvest.

What are your thorns and thistle in life? Is it a new weed in your garden, a virus on your computer, an inability to deliver services as promised, interoffice conflicts, employees who forget to follow correct procedures, customers angry about what you haven't done, or a lack of communication between upper and middle management? The list of pesky problems that threaten our work is endless, and we must vigilantly be on guard to keep these pests tended. If left untended these little problems can infest and destroy our work.

Pain, sweat, and tending the thorns and thistle are all part of the difficulty that we are going to encounter in work, and we must prepare to battle through these difficulties. Now some may say that pointing out these difficulties will only breed a pessimistic attitude and low expectations in work, but it is vital to deal with these realities. Acknowledging this difficulty and reflecting upon it "has nothing to do with pessimism. It is sober realism which excludes any idealism of human work."[5] If we have an idealized or unrealistic expectation in work, we will be easy prey to discouragement and surrender when the difficulties of work kick us in the face. Our culture is one that quits as soon as things get hard, and if we are going to succeed in work it is only going to be by pressing through difficulties. If we think success will come through anything but hard work then we are destined for failure. The natural and normal path to a harvest is one that involves strenuous work, much pain, and the taming of many prickly thorns and thistle.

5.3 All Fields of Work Are Infected

I remember experiencing the harsh realities of the curse one day in college while studying in the library for a Chemistry final. The concepts were not fitting into my brain, and when they did get in they didn't stay long. I had to look at them again and again and again. As I was doing this, I finally realized the theory of entropy that I was studying described my situation. The theory of entropy basically states that everything tends to disorder. As a result of the curse, things fall apart. Customers get mad, orders get lost, sprinklers break, copiers get jammed, and concepts disappear from my mind. Everything tends to disorder. No matter what profession we are in it will take great effort through painful, sweaty toil (even in a library) to reap a harvest.

No field of work is spared this disordering effect of the fall. Allan Richardson connects the idea of entropy to the entirety of the world calling it "the cosmic disarrangement of things which result from rebellion against God's will."[6] Seeing the curse as a cosmic disarrangement helps us recognize it affects everything. All things get thorns and thistle and resist subduing. All forms of work have been infected by this virus.

---

[5] Claus Westermann, *Genesis,* vol 1 (Mineapolis: Fortress Press, 1994), 265.

[6] Allan Richardson, *The Biblical Doctrine of Work* (London: SCM Press, 1952), 24.

The disarranging effects of the curse are going to hinder no matter what type of vocation we are in. As we get acquainted with the thorns, thistle, sweat, and pain of a particular industry or profession, it can become easy to think other fields are greener, less difficult, and less affected by the curse. The cosmic element reminds there is no way to escape the curse by fleeing to another industry, company, or product.

We must not buy into the lure of false promises that offer work with no curse. These promises come in the form of a new miracle product, a great paying job that requires little effort, a new technology that will make our wildest dreams come true, or a new book that guarantees instant success. Such things come with curse-defying claims that are false and misleading. People flock to these only to have the harsh reality of the curse come crashing down on them later. Such claims are untrue and their deceitful promises must be resisted.

Some jobs may certainly be better than others, but ultimately all are done under the curse. It is not just agricultural fields that are corrupted, but as John Calvin said "the whole order was subverted by the sin of man."[7] There will be times where "better opportunities" arise, but all work suffers the curse, and we must not be duped by false claims. As long as we are in this life, there will be no complete escape from disarranging effects of the curse.

5.4 The Greater the Goal the Greater the Difficulty

Tommy was a sales manager for an entry level position and was in search of a way to motivate his new reps. He decided to show them their opportunity to make as much money as they wanted. He asked what income each wanted to make and after determining this he would work backward to show how many deals they would need to close each day to get that income, then how many appointments they would need to set each day to close that amount of deals, and then how many new prospects they would need to find each day to set that many appointments. After

---

[7] Calvin, *Calvin's Commentaries*, vol 1, 177.

going through some very realistic goals, his reps began asking about larger incomes. They began asking for more lofty goals and didn't stop until they saw the projections for what the top one percent of reps in the company were making. To his surprise all the reps wrote down this lofty number and left to "go make it happen." Tommy's tactic worked to motivate his reps that day, but a year later none had achieved the goal. A few were making an average income but most were still below average. What happened?

The problem was that the work was hard and their lofty goals would not come easily. They needed to figure out how to do their job effectively and overcome its obstacles. For many it seemed the more business they brought in the more problems (thorns and thistle) they had. The more they sold the more customer complaints and service issues came up. They found their lofty goals very difficult to attain.

It's hard to be good at a job, harder to be above average, and extremely difficult to be the very best. There is an increasing difficulty with increasingly great achievement. The philosopher Plato was quoted with a saying that in Greek was "duskola ta kala,"[8] which literally means things are "difficult according to the good." That is things that are excellent are also arduous and difficult.[9] The loftier the goal the harder it is. It's hard to run a small company and even harder to run a billion dollar company. It's hard to do well in school and even harder to do well in pre-med classes. It's hard to lead a small group Bible study and harder to lead an entire church. It's hard to be a quarterback in high school and even harder in the NFL. It's hard to succeed in a job and even harder to influence multitudes through it. The grander the goal the more difficult it is. With greater goals come more arduous obstacles.

As we seek to do great things for the Lord, we should not be surprised to find those great goals hard to achieve. People want influential positions, but are not willing to work more than forty hours. They want to be a doctor and heal others, but they are not willing to study on the weekend. They want to evangelize the

---

[8] John Calvin, *Calvin's Commentary*, vol XXI (Grand Rapids: Baker Books, 2009), 73. Commentary on 1 Tim 3:1
[9] Ibid.

world, but they don't want ridicule from the man next door. They want the big job title but they are not willing to be great at their current job. Work is hard and the greater the achievement desired the greater the difficulty to achieve that goal. Nothing worthwhile ever comes easily. No one will ever have greatness simply handed to them; they must be willing to work hard and overcome big obstacles.

The fact that lofty goals are hard should not deter us from going after them, but rather it should inform us that those lofty goals will not come easily. Everything good is also difficult to acquire. People too quickly give up on great goals and assume the Lord has not called them simply because they experience big hurdles. If great goals are to be achieved great obstacles will have to be overcome.

5.5 Don't be Surprised By the Difficulty

This chapter on the curse is not intended to discourage us, but rather to help us see the cost required to overcome it. When building a house we first estimate the cost, same thing happens before a president declares war, or before one decides to follow Jesus (Luke 14:25-33). It is important to know success comes at great effort, so that we are not overwhelmed or surprised when difficulty comes. This chapter should prepare us for the hard battle ahead. In a similar way the apostle Peter wrote to suffering Christians to explain that they would indeed suffer in the world. He told them "Do not be surprised at the painful trial you are suffering, as though something strange were happening to you" (1 Peter 4:12). In the midst of trials it is easy to think something strange or wrong is happening, and the difficulties of work are no different.

Many people today think life is supposed to be easy, and if it isn't something is wrong. Christians often think that we are supposed to come to Jesus and all our troubles will disappear, or that we find God's path when everything magically falls into place for us. This is not true. There are going to be trials for everyone to some degree or another, even when following God wholeheartedly, and we need to be prepared to press through these.

The tendency to be surprised by difficulty often leads to giving up. This is particularly common for young people who grow discouraged and quit as soon as things get hard. The fact that things don't go easily or success is not immediate does not mean you are in the wrong profession or will never succeed in that job. There is a time to evaluate if you are in the right position, but more than likely if you are in a job and not sure of success you probably just need to work harder. People give up far too easily today.

When I was struggling at my first sales job I found great encouragement talking to a very successful friend and hearing how early in his career he was close to getting fired for poor performance. It took him a long time to figure out his job and how to effectively overcome difficulties. With time, determination, and much effort he began to slowly experience success. Hearing his story helped me realize there was hope. Success does not happen overnight, and some of the best lessons are learned in the most difficult times. History is filled with great figures who didn't give up in difficulties, and many of those we share offices with can give testimonies of persevering in difficulty. Often the problem is not the difficulty but the fact that we want success with no effort or pain, and that is not the way it comes. We must see the importance of not giving up when things get hard.

In addition to giving up, the surprise of difficulty can also lead to bitterness. We get angry because things are hard. Embittered people get mad at other people or things and say things they shouldn't (they even throw shovels on the ground). They feel squeezed by difficulties and in turn squeeze others. The daily grind wears them out and after focusing only on the pain and hardships they soon have no joy, hope, or excitement. They anticipate only bad things to come.

In elementary school I had a friend whose father would come home from work each day angry. After getting out of the car, his only words to his two sons were harsh and degrading commands as he made his way into the house to get a beer. As a result of his attitude, his sons quit calling him dad and nicknamed him Grump Lord (which needless to say did not improve the situation). Our circumstances may not be exactly the same as his, and we may hide or express bitterness in differing ways, but if we do not have the right perspective on the difficulties of life we stand prone to become Grump Lords—those who have been embittered and in turn seek to embitter others.

No one becomes a Grump Lord over night; it comes by constant wear and tear of an embittered soul that has not been nourished by the hope of the grace of God. Hebrews 12:15 says "See to it that no one misses the grace of God and that no bitter root grows up to cause trouble and defile many." Just as we watch our business to make sure thorns and thistle do not grow, we should also tend our souls to make sure no roots of bitterness choke out our joy and hope.

We should not be surprised or lose hope when difficulties come. Everyone is going to experience defeats. There are going to be times it's hard, times you fail, times you step out in faith and fall on your face. There will be times you make a terrible decision, times you miscalculate the cost, times where you do everything right, and it still doesn't go your way. Even times where you think Hell has just unleashed all of its demons upon you. These are part of life under the curse and not something strange and unusual, therefore we should not give up or get angry when they come. We must continue to fight focused on the chief goal.

5.6 A Goal Worth Fighting For

Randy was an engineer enjoying the completion of a major project. He had poured a lot of hard work into this project, and he was finally finished. He decided now it was time to kick back and enjoy life. He had been through a lot, and it was time for him to have no hard work or painful surprises. Life was going to be easy!

This seemed like a promising plan, but it quickly changed. It changed when he picked up his Bible and read Matthew 25:14-30. He realized God had given him gifts to use, and he was sobered by the unfaithful servant in the story, who instead of putting his talent to use hid it because his master was hard. This servant was called wicked and lazy. Randy suddenly realized it was his own laziness leading him to neglect his gifts and his Master's glory.

Like Randy, many people today seek after ease and comfort and in doing so they neglect to use their God given gifts. The glory of God is worth pursuing above all other things, and that includes ease. If we value something, then we ought to be willing to pay a price for it (Matt 13:44). If we stop pursuing something because of a little difficulty then we don't really value what is being pursued. If the kingdom of God is worth selling all we have to acquire, then it is also worth enduring hardship. If we love God and want to honor him with our talents, then we should be willing to take on challenges and do hard things. We have a goal and kingdom that is well worth working hard for.

In John Bunyan's classic book *The Pilgrims Progress,* the main character Christian is asked why his companion named Pliable abandoned him at the slough of despond while they were on their journey to the Celestial City. Christian tells them it was because of the difficulty and another inquires, "Is the celestial glory of so small esteem with him that he counts it not worth running the hazards of a few difficulties to obtain it?"[10] Bunyan's question is insightfully revealing, and we should ask if we value God's glory enough to endure a few hazards.

5.7 Working With Faith

The hardship of work is important to understand, but hardship shouldn't be the only way we view work. There are many reasons for entering into work with much faith. Even in the curse there resides a hint at success that should inspire us. Genesis 3:19 says "by the sweat of your brow you will eat." The curse shows it takes much effort to eat, but it does say we will eat. The curse makes work difficult but not impossible, and we need to enter into work aware of difficulties but full of faith for accomplishing things.

An important passage that helps us see stability in work is God's covenant with Noah. God destroyed the world because of its wickedness, but saved Noah and afterward said in Genesis 8:22 says, "As long as the earth endures, seedtime and harvest, cold and heat, summer and winter, day and night will never cease." Instead of future destruction God shows the earth will be "blessed with the

---

[10] John Bunyan, *The Pilgrims Progress* (New York: Penguin, 1987), 26.

regularity of predictable environmental patterns that are undergirded by the directive hand of God."[11] God binds the chaos and establishes stable patterns that make it possible to work in a consistent and predictable manner. The use of opposite terms in this verse like summer and winter, cold and heat, day and night is a figure of speech known as a merism, which places opposites together to show the all-encompassing nature of each. These opposites function to show the all-inclusive nature of the pattern—it means all the time. God establishes patterns that are timely and predictable and give security to the world and its inhabitants.[12]

This means we can expect consistent patterns in work that fairly predictably lead to harvests, profits, and completed goals. Work may be difficult, but it is not impossible. We should be ready to engage in work knowing God has ordered the world so that hard work usually leads to profit. He has not abandoned the world to utter chaos. We embark into work mindful of the difficulty but full of faith that success is possible. God has limited the difficulty so that we can live and work effectively.

We should also have faith because as Calvin said, God "sprinkles everywhere tokens of his goodness." We see God's goodness unexpectedly interrupt our days to meet our needs. His goodness is consistently experienced and this is what led David to exclaim "the earth is full of the mercy of God" (Psalm 33:5)."[13] The obstacles of the curse are often the very places we see God's gracious provision, and this should fill us with faith. Though the sprinkler breaks, we eventually get it fixed. Though the printer jams at the most critical moment, an alternative is usually found. Though the computer dies in the midst of the most important presentation, or it's another of many days with a Grump Lord of a client, God's grace usually provides a way to overcome. We may be hard pressed but we are never in despair (2 Cor 4:8). In all the difficulties of life, God's tokens of grace provide for us, so that even in the darkest situation rays of God's light dawn. God's stable

---

[11] Mathews, K. A. *Genesis 1-11:26*, (Nashville: Broadman & Holman Publishers, 2001), 396.

[12] Ibid, 397. This is a close paraphrase.

[13] John Calvin, *Calvin's Commentaries,* vol 1, 173-4.

world and his constant provision should inspire us to work with
faith in the midst of all our difficulty.

5.8 The Curse Broken

Working through thorns and thistles is what causes gray
hairs and mis-proportioned bodies, but the curse has a much
bleaker end than these. The curse brings death, and contemplating
God's stable world will not keep it from stalking us down. If the
difficulties of this world can leave us weary and bitter then
certainly the inescapable reality of death could push us to complete
despair, or as Allan Richardson said, our inability to deliver
ourselves should drive us "to seek for one who saves from sin and
redeems the whole of human life."[14] Our greatest need is not just
provision in the midst of the curse but the removal of the curse.

Sin is serious. It is rebellion to God, and it is the reason for
such a weighty curse. We have disobeyed a holy and perfect God,
and as painful as our difficulties in this life may be the ultimate
end of the curse is not just physical death but spiritual death—that
is eternal death. It is eternal separation from a holy God. Sin
deserves eternal punishment. Our greatest need is not a bonus or
promotion, but rather the forgiveness of sins.

The greatest sign of God's grace comes in providing for our
greatest need. It is him sending his Son Jesus Christ to die for our
sins so that we might be saved from the curse. Jesus took the
punishment sin deserved so that sinners could experience what the
righteous deserve. In speaking of this great exchange F.F Bruce
said of Christ, "In his death everything was made His that sin had
made ours."[15] The sinless Savior took the full punishment for sin
so that we might have the promise of eternal life.

Phillip Ryken said, "If we are to be saved, the curse must
be removed. And this is what Christ was doing on the cross:
redeeming his people from the law's accursed penalty."[16] The

---

[14] Richardson, 27.

[15] F.F. Bruce, *The Epistle to Galatia*, Grand Rapids: Eerdmans, 1982), 166.

[16] Phillip Ryken, *Galatians* (Phillipsburg: P&R, 2005), 114.

world we live in is ravaged by the fall, but because of Christ we can anticipate a day where the curse is totally removed. Though the curse's lingering effects still remain, its power has been broken and a new day awaits those who trust in Christ. This hope is what can sweeten all our trials. No matter how bitter a cup we may drink right now we know it is not the fullness we deserve, and there is no dark difficulty that the hope of the gospel cannot overcome.

There are two important ways Christ breaking the power of the curse influences how we confront the curse in daily life. First, when we taste the bitterness of the curse it should remind of the offensiveness of sin. Sin is serious and that is why Jesus had to die. When we question the pain of the curse or ask, "Why does it have to be so hard?" we are questioning the severity of our offense against a holy God. We bear a bitter curse because we made a great offense. Secondly, the seriousness of sin helps us see how great the work of Christ is. It is his work we trust and hope in. He took the brunt of the curse so we might never have to experience its fullness. Seeing the severity of the penalty helps us marvel in the deliverance. The curse will not have the last word. Its power is now broken, and we anticipate a new day with no more curse. It is the work of a Savior who suffered the curse and broke its power that gives us hope and confidence in all our trials.

5.8 The Ultimate Pay Day

Most people are willing to jump through hurdles, endure setbacks, face a little pain, and work tirelessly if they are paid enough. When you get a paycheck at the end of the week often you sit back and think, "It was worth it." And there are other times we think, "No way I worked that hard for so little!" When we are tempted to second guess continuing in difficult work we need to remember the eternal reward God has for his faithful servants. God has a glorious pay day in store for those who trust in Christ, and we now turn to look at it. Revelation 21 and 22 points us to this day, and we do well to remember it:

> And I heard a loud voice from the throne saying, "Now the dwelling of God is with men, and he will live with them.

They will be his people, and God himself will be with them and be their God. He will wipe every tear from their eyes. There will be no more death or mourning or crying or pain, for the old order of things has passed away."
Revelation 21:3-5

Then the angel showed me the river of the water of life, as clear as crystal, flowing from the throne of God and of the Lamb down the middle of the great street of the city. On each side of the river stood the tree of life, bearing twelve crops of fruit, yielding its fruit every month. And the leaves of the tree are for the healing of the nations. No longer will there be any curse. The throne of God and of the Lamb will be in the city, and his servants will serve him. They will see his face, and his name will be on their foreheads. There will be no more night. They will not need the light of a lamp or the light of the sun, for the Lord God will give them light. And they will reign forever and ever.
Revelation 22:1-5

These verses show the wonderful news of the new heavens and earth. All the pain and difficulties endured will be wiped away. Nothing will be cursed. There will be no more difficulty of the ground, painful toil, evil, or strife. It is a new order characterized by joy, peace, and abundance. As difficulties are experienced in this life, it should lead to rejoicing for the day when they are no more. All the difficulties, all the things that go wrong, all the unexpected mishaps, all the attacks of evil people, all the hardships, and all the pain should point you to a new day.

Since being a Christian there have been few things that increased my desired for heaven more than realizing what life would be like with no curse. The earth will no longer be cursed to bind in with obstacles. There will be no difference between the order of the world and that of heaven. Heaven and earth will be of one accord and will sing the same song. The pains felt now will be no more. You will no longer survive by the sweat of your brow. The order of life will not be as it was in the garden but better (for Satan and evil will not be there!), and we will see God face to face. It will be delightful. Those pains you now feel, those tears you have shed when you felt like God had you in a vice and was squeezing you from all sides will be wiped away with the bliss of heaven. The curse will be gone and the places thorns and thistle once grew will be marked by blessing upon blessing. It will be a time of great joy for the entire world. The anticipation of this future joy should also add joy to our work and trials now.

Since the removal of the curse and its effects will bring an age of great joy, it is only appropriate to end this chapter with a song. The song choice may initially strike you, but I hope it will cause you to reflect on what the words really mean in whatever season we hear it. And hopefully it will help connect our curse and difficulties to our Savior and deliverance.

The song is *Joy to the World*, and though it is typically associated with Christmas and the incarnation, the song is really about Christ's second coming. It is when the Lord *is* come and the nature of the earth is changed to be like that of heaven. It is about Christ being present in this new order—heaven on earth. A time where there will be no more curse, no more sorrows, no thorns, no thistle, no cosmic disarrangement, and all creation will joyously proclaim the glory of the king. Those who trust in Christ and prepare him room in their hearts will experience the flow of his blessing. The hope expressed in this song should inspire us to do work that matters—that is work that presses through difficulties and prepares the earth to receive her king.

> Joy to the world, the Lord is come
> Let earth receive her King
> Let every heart prepare Him room
> And heaven and nature sing
> And heaven and nature sing
> And heaven, and nature sing
>
> Joy to the earth, the Savior reigns
> Let men their songs employ
> While fields and floods
> Rocks, hills and plains
> Repeat the sounding joy
> Repeat the sounding joy
> Repeat, repeat the sounding joy

No more let sins and sorrows grow
Nor thorns infest the ground
He comes to make His blessing flow
Far as the curse is found
Far as the curse is found
Far as, far as the curse is found

He rules the world with truth and grace
And makes the nations prove
The glories of His righteousness
And wonders of His love
And wonders of His love
And wonders, of His love

Chapter 5 Discussion Questions

1. What are your greatest obstacles at work?

2. Where are you tempted to give up or grow bitter in your work?

3. How has God provided for you and helped you overcome difficulties and obstacles in the past?

4. What verses help you trust God in the midst of difficult work?

Chapter 6

Disappointments—Persevering with Faith and Hope

"How long, O LORD? Will you forget me forever?
How long will you hide your face from me?
How long must I wrestle with my thoughts and every day have
sorrow in my heart?
How long will my enemy triumph over me?
Look on me and answer, O LORD my God.
Give light to my eyes, or I will sleep in death...
But I trust in your unfailing love;
my heart rejoices in your salvation."
Psalm 13:1-3, 5

Jason pulled into the parking lot near his office, turned the car engine off, laid his head on the steering wheel, and in desperation said to himself "I can't take another day of this!" He had always worked hard hoping to set himself up for a great job at a major corporation, but now found himself working in a call center and barely making ends meet.

He gave up a dream opportunity to be closer to family and was then passed over time and time again, for various reasons, at various jobs. He was too qualified for some, not qualified enough for others. Finally he took this job as a "temporary fix" to make ends meet. The weeks turned to months and the months to years.

Today was yet another day he debated going in. The car door felt like it weighed a hundred pounds, but having no alternatives he pushed it open, and began the long walk to his cubicle. He spent most of his days thinking of all the reasons he shouldn't be there, and trying hard to work faithfully at a job he wished he didn't have. He didn't like his situation, but no matter how much he tried he couldn't get out. He was in despair and didn't know what to do or how to think about his situation.

Working in a call center is not a bad job, but it was not what Jason had trained and longed to do, and for that reason he struggled being there. Like Jason, most people will experience some degree of disappointment in their career aspirations. Work is a great and glorious task God calls us to, but because it is done under the curse there will be disappointments. These disappointments are not just the daily difficulties of work; they are prolonged and pronounced hardships that last for seasons.

Such disappointing seasons are not unusual. They are common to us today, and they were common to those in the Bible. For example, Moses was called by God to deliver the Israelites from the hand of the Egyptians, and when he first took the task upon himself it was in an effort to stop a fight. He ended up killing an Egyptian and soon found himself fleeing to save his own life. This promising deliverer would end up fleeing the royal palace and spending years tending sheep as a nomad—no doubt a disappointing job transition!

There is also Paul who set out on his famous missionary journey to strengthen churches and preach the gospel in places he had not yet been, but his journey didn't take the steps most of us would envision. Paul quickly experienced opposition and was arrested, beaten, and thrown in prison for his teaching.

King David's life also had its disappointing seasons. God called the prophet Samuel to anoint David king over Israel, but the problem was that Israel already had a king—Saul. David would have to wait for the demise of Saul before ascending to the throne. There were times David served as Saul's armor bearer and harpist, and other times he would have to run for his life from Saul. And like Moses, he too held the transitional job of herding sheep.

Joseph is another person familiar with disappointments. He showed great aptitude at a young age but was sold into slavery by his jealous brothers. He later rose to prominence by becoming an attendant to Potiphar, a high ranking Egyptian official, but he was again betrayed, this time by the lies of a woman, and thrown in prison for an offense he did not commit.

Disappointments are common to all. No one is free from suffering them. D.A. Carson has said all we have to do is live long enough and we will suffer.[1] This is true in life, and it is true in work. There will be times when we are fired from a job, when we are unable to get the position we want, when a lucrative job goes south, when we are not having the God-glorifying influence we anticipated, or when it seems like no matter what we do we cannot climb out of the position we are in. Just because we are working to glorify God does not mean there will not be setbacks. All work is done under the curse, and as everyone experiences the difficulties of the curse, everyone will also experience disappointing seasons, and for that reason we must now consider how to persevere through these times.

6.1 Common Ways Disappointments are Encountered in Work

Everyone has hopes and dreams for their careers, but the difficulties of life can hinder, delay, and even destroy those dreams. "Hope deferred makes the heart sick" (Proverbs 13:12), and when our desires are not realized it can lead to frustration, depression, and disappointment; all evidences of a sick heart. The disappointments of Moses and David came through herding sheep, and while herding isn't what most people struggle with today, there are some similarities.

There will be times we are out of work and struggle just to find a job, but disappointments in work will involve more than being unemployed. The most basic components of ideal work that we would all like to have are: 1) working in a job that fits our gifting (Rom 12:6-8), 2) working at what we enjoy or are passionate about (Ecc 3:22), and 3) earning enough profit to make ends meet (2 Thess 3:10).[2] These core components have a biblical and practical precedence and are what everyone desires. Most of our prolonged difficulty at work will occur when one of these basic

---

[1] D.A. Carson, *How long O Lord* (Grand Rapids: Baker Book House, 1990), 69.
[2] Jim Collins has a helpful critique on what he calls his hedgehog concept of the three essential things for companies need to do to be successful. I think this corresponds to biblical criteria for individual work. Jim Collins, *Good to Great* (New York: Harper Collins, 2001), 96.

components is lacking or absent. Here are a few examples that highlight the importance of each.

Todd got a job on Wall Street making six figures right out of college. He was great at giving high level presentations and was making unbelievable money, but the cutthroat out-to-get-you environment of his office began to take away from his enjoyment. Though he was making great money, he began to struggle in that environment and longed to be at a company he was excited to represent.

Brian was a great computer programmer, but because of reorganization in the office he was moved into management. His new job paid well, and he liked directing people, but he was not very good at it. He frequently found himself the cause of bottle necks and miscommunications. He felt inadequate and underutilized in this role and longed to work where he was most gifted and effective.

Scott was a contractor working on a large, long-term, and lucrative project. Midway through the project he realized his team made significant mistakes and would have to redo much of their work. The lucrative project turned into a money pit. At best the long project would be a breakeven deal, and he struggled showing up day after day to work on job that was paying nothing.

We may experience many different combinations and degrees of disappointment. There will be times we endure a low grade disappoint for years, because even though we don't especially enjoy our job, we continue in it because we have gifts for it and it pays the bills. We may have more significant disappointments when we have a job we don't enjoy, are not good at, and can't get by on its income. There may also be intense difficulties when the business we mortgaged the house to finance fails, and we lose everything. There are many varieties and many degrees of disappointment at work, but the majority of challenging seasons revolve around these core components.

These components of ideal work inform where struggles often lie, and it is wise to let them shape career decisions and preparation. When choosing a career people often focus on one area to the detriment of others. Some choose a profession, because it pays great without considering if they are gifted for it. Others choose the high paying job without considering how enjoyable it is. Others pursue careers that are fun without considering if they will actually provide. As we pursue careers, wisdom sees the importance of these and considers how to assure their presence in work.

We can take measures to improve the likelihood of having a job with these components, but there is no silver bullet approach. At times regardless of how well we plan, there will still be disappointments, because some disappointment is inevitable in a fallen world. Since not all disappointments can be prevented, we now consider how to persevere when it does come.

6.2 Persevering Toward the Goal

Disappointment can lead to a prison of unfaithful and uninspired work. It prevents us from glorifying God and doing the necessary things to get out of the disappointing situation. Our culture is one that crumbles under the weight of unmet expectations, and we need to have a faith that doesn't buckle with such disappointment. There are four things we can do to keep from crumbling in these times.

1. Focus on the Ultimate Goal

The chief end of man is to glorify God, and as we have seen, work provides an opportunity to achieve this end. Everything we do provides an opportunity to bring God glory, and the disappointing seasons are no different. These seasons may be disappointing to us, and we may not be where we would like to be honoring God, but it is still an opportunity to bring him glory and store up treasures in heaven. Though our hopes of a great career have been deferred, it does not mean the ultimate goal has been lost. The ability to achieve this goal in any circumstance should temper our disappointment.

Suppose a person's chief goal for the next five years is to make a million dollars, and he is currently an engineer. If his chief goal is making a million dollars, should he be upset if he is fired and takes a job as a janitor making $200,000 a year? His chief goal has been met, so he should be rejoicing regardless of his job title.

Likewise, if our goal really is to honor God we should rejoice at any opportunity that allows us to achieve that goal.

These seasons provide a unique opportunity to demonstrate to the world that God is more important to us than the ideal job, and that he is worthy to be glorified even when things don't go our way. Our hope in life is based on Jesus' death and resurrection, not our ability to secure a comfortable life. We serve God not to get what we want, but because he is God. These times can reveal why we truly serve God, and telling others we will serve him even if stripped of the essentials of life can have a profound impact.

Focusing on the chief goal also allows us to work with faith, hope, and joy. It transforms our attitude. We work diligently and faithfully not because of what we receive now, but because it honors God, and we know we will receive a reward for this on the day we stand before him. We work because it honors him. This should drive us to do great things even in perilous situations, and it also seems to be what drove the actions of many biblical figures, and led them to become heroes of faith, rather than depressed workers.

Paul was beaten and imprisoned on his missionary journey, and rather than giving up because of misfortune, he was compelled to glorify God. After his beating, he was singing hymns and praising God in prison when a violent earthquake shook the building and the doors flew open. When the nearby guard realized the prisoners would now escape he moved to kill himself. But instead of fleeing to save himself, Paul acted to save the guard's life. The guard then exclaimed "What must I do to be saved?" (Acts 16:30). He and his whole family believed and were baptized into the faith. The success of Paul's mission did not come the way he may have envisioned it, but focusing on the chief goal created opportunities that many would have missed, and Paul was able to do the very thing he had set off to do. Paul did not see prison as a setback, but as an opportunity to glorify God. He saw the opportunity in the disappointing time and made the most of it (Eph 5:16).

In his rise to power David did not waiver in his faith nor did he try to take matters into his own hands. He trusted God and served Saul. David actually had opportunities to kill Saul, which would have given him the throne immediately, yet he would not do it. His trust was in God, and he was more interested in honoring God than achieving a position.

In difficult times Joseph was faithful with whatever was put before him. He was ready to interpret dreams that troubled fellow prisons. Faith in the living God seems to be what gave him the confidence to do this. His faithfulness was first and foremost to God Joseph and that enabled him to be faithful to those around him. He trusted God through setbacks and believed God's hand was with him through it all. Joseph was seventeen when sold into slavery by his brothers, and he was thirty when he entered the service of Pharaoh. His trust and faith through these thirteen years of abandonment, prison, and disappointment prompted him to do great work even when it went against all reason. Focusing on God seems to be what allowed him to persevere through very difficult circumstances.

Each of these men faced unusual setbacks and disappointments and in them they demonstrated unusual faith and hope. The chief motivating factor seems to be a great passion to honor God. They served him not to get what they wanted out of life, but because he was God, and worthy to be worshiped. It is common to see people have set backs, but what is rare is seeing people pressing on, not giving up, and working with all their heart. These men demonstrated a great faith that was not tied to earthly circumstances. Martin Luther said, "Faith moves life's center from earth to heaven. When the center is moved, the burden that falls upon us on earth appears in another light."[3] These men showed their hope was not on earth but in heaven, and their faith was in a God who was far greater than their trials. Faith moved the focus to the eternal throne in heaven, and it allowed them to see their struggles and setbacks through an entirely different lens.

2. **Trust in God's Dominion**

It is always good and right to remind ourselves that ultimately we are not in control of our lives. God is. It is helpful to

---

[3] Gustaf Wingren, *Luther on Vocation,* (Eugene: Wipf and Stock, 1957), 235.

remember this when experiencing success, so we don't become proud, and when experiencing disappointment, so we don't become discouraged. God is the one reigning over everything, and all his attributes, especially his dominion and goodness, should encourage us in difficulties. His dominion reminds that he is sovereign over all things, and his goodness reminds that he works everything for our benefit. In seasons of prolonged disappointment it is tempting to think we have fallen to a state beyond the reach of God's control and that we have no hope. D.A. Carson said, "God's sovereignty functions to assure us things are not getting out of control."[4] Since nothing is outside of God's control, we should trust him in all seasons.

God was fully present and aware that Joseph was in prison. In fact, being in prison, and not just any prison, but the very prison where Pharaoh's servants were confined (Gen 39:20) was the means by which Joseph would ascend to the king's right hand. God was in control, and even in this difficult situation, "where no man could imagine it, God had all the strings in his hand."[5] God does not work vindictively or even arbitrarily; he works all things for the good of those who love him (Rom 8:28).

It is important to recognize these truths, because often in trials we only see the hands of others at work. It may be the hands that sold us into slavery, the hands that threw us in prison, or the hands that promised a promotion only to change their mind. Jerry Bridges said, "Above all, (God's sovereignty) will give us the confidence that no plan of God's can be thwarted by either human actions or acts of nature."[6] In the midst, and often in spite of the evil intentions or forgotten promises of others, God's good and sovereign purpose is resolutely moving forward.

When God's sovereignty is understood it teaches us to trust him and his moving. God is the one who raises people up. Psalm 75:6-7 says, "No one from the east or the west or from the desert can exalt a man. But it is God who judges: He brings one down, he

---

[4] Carson, 239.

[5] Gerhard von Rad, *Genesis,* Old Testament Library (Philadelphia: Westminster Press, 1972), 432.

[6] Jerry Bridges, "Does Divine Sovereignty Make a Difference in Every Day Life" in Bruce Ware and Thomas R. Shreiner, editors, *Still Sovereign* (Grand Rapids: Baker Books, 2003), 306.

exalts another." The rising and falling of people is in God's hand, and we must trust his decisions. We focus on being faithful to him, and we wait for his moving. It is humbling, but we must recognize with Os Guinness, "All the will in the world may not make us what we want to become."[7] We are dependent on God, and we must trust his governing of the world.

Trusting God also means we wait on his timing, which is one of the great difficulties in disappointment. If we knew when the trial would end we would be fine to endure. It is not our thoughts that rule. "God must give everything its time." [8] Though we labor in disappointment we trust that in the right season God will change our circumstances. Just as we wait for the right season to pick watermelons or apples, so also we must wait for the right season for the right job opportunity.[9]

In these times we need to trust God with what is in his control, while still being faithful with the responsibility he gives to us. To do this it is important to separate the sphere of God's responsibility and the sphere of our responsibility. This is pictured below in Figure 1.

In work, we must be faithful with what God entrusts to us, and trust him for what only he can do. We sow the seed and water it, but God makes it grow (1 Cor 3:6). We labor for revenue, but only God brings it. We work to win the business, but God directs the customers heart (Prov 21:1). We knock on the door for a job, but God opens it. We build the business, but God blesses it. Understanding God's responsibility and our responsibilities can alter how we walk through difficulties.

---

[7] Os Guiness, *The Call* (Nashville: Tom Nelson, 2003), *23*.
[8] Wingren, 216.
[9] Ibid. This is based off a similar illustration by Wingren.

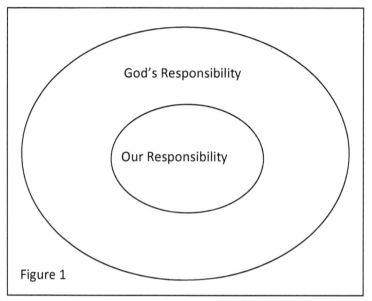

Figure 1

When we labor faithfully and miss the promotion there is peace we are doing what should be done. When we are being faithful, and yet lose money, we trust him. When we are faithful to look for a new job, but none comes open, we trust in his provision. Many people struggle with joy and patience in difficulties because they think they are responsible for God's duties. Others blame God when it is actually their unfaithful performance or unwise actions that prolong their misfortune (Pro 19:3). Understanding these different responsibilities can keep us from being irresponsible with what is in our control or overly responsible with what is in His control. We must focus on what we can do, while fully trusting God with what is beyond our ability.

3. Faithful Even In Small Things

When we know God has us where we are, and that we have not happened there by chance, it leads to being faithful in that

---

[10]Paul David Tripp, *Instruments of Change* (Philipsburg: P&R Publishing, 2002), 250.

place, even with undesirable jobs. Our responsibility is to be faithful with what God entrusts to us through his sovereign care. Our goal is not to become a millionaire or CEO, but to hear "Well done, good and faithful servant" (Matt 25:21).

Part of the difficulty in disappointments is having to be faithful with little things. Jason was not disappointed because his career turned and he ended up managing billion dollar accounts. It's that he was working with insignificant matters: small things that "anybody could do."

Even small tasks require great skill to do well. We must prove competent with small things before anyone will trust us with big things. It is said of David that whatever Saul sent him to do he did it successfully (1 Sam 18:5). This gives a glimpse into David's being a man after God's own heart, and how he did everything, even the "insignificant jobs" with a focus on honoring God. The result of this was that Saul promoted him to "a high rank."

Those who learn to overcome the obstacles in a fallen world and show an aptitude in small things will likely overcome obstacles when the stakes are higher. It is a contradiction to think you will be faithful with grand things when you are failing with the small things. Lowly positions provide an opportunity to learn to work effectively to overcome the curse and all its difficulties, and this can have a direct transference to faithfully handling great things.

It is easy to think we are great at our jobs and question why God has not advanced us. In reality we do better to pay more attention to handling our responsibility well. If we are faithful with what is before us, we can give a good account to God, and a natural byproduct of faithful work is that those around us take notice and give us more responsibility. By focusing on being faithful to God, you may end up like Joseph who in one day went from being in prison to governing the greatest nation of his time.

It takes time to learn to do any job well, and many hurt themselves by too quickly leaving one job for another opportunity. It is far better to do one job well than bounce around doing many jobs poorly. In describing the advantage of focusing on one job, Plato said "all things are produced more plentifully and easily and of a better quality, when one man does one thing which is natural to him."[11] By seeking to master one job, rather than jumping around, we increase the chances of being faithful to that job. When we learn more about one job we become more effective at it, which can also make it more enjoyable and profitable. Unfortunately today people often change jobs before they really learn to do it well.

Faithfulness in small things normally leads to being entrusted with more, and it is often what God uses to pull people out of disappointments. It is a consistent pattern in the men we have looked at and is a natural part of life. As we are faithful, we should anticipate opportunities opening up. When we can demonstrate great skill in a job it naturally increases the demand for our skills. This should encourage us to think positively in disappointment and encourage us to be diligent workers.

It is important to think positively in these times, but positive thinking is not the main goal. I want to promote a deep and abiding trust in God, who is good, who desires to do you good, who has ordained your setbacks, and who could at any moment cause the wind to fill your sails and make you go in directions and places you could never have dreamed. But the faith and trust I am calling for says, "God, if you never cause the wind to blow, and I sit in the shallow end of the pond never going where I hoped, still I will be faithful and happy as long as I am with you." Until we can be content and faithful in the place where we are, we are not ready for the fierce wind to blow. Only when we learn to love success not for itself but for how it could glorify God are we ready to work for true glory.

Such an attitude understands God's glory is the goal, and that he positions you where he wants you to glorify him. Recognizing it is his hand that brings every opportunity builds trust and reminds success is not about getting where we want but being faithful with what he has set before you. Being primarily concerned with giving the Lord a good account will keep us working with excellence and vigilance in the midst of difficulties. And very often our faithfulness in disappointing jobs leads to new opportunities that may very well end our disappointing season.

---

[11] Plato, *Republic,* trans Robin Waterfield (Oxford: Oxford University Press, 1993), 370c.

4. Press into God

Martin Luther taught that troubles and tribulations are to bring us closer to God; they benefit rather than harm us.[12] This however, can only happen when we encounter them with faith. A significant struggle for us in seasons of disappointment is summed up by Martin Lloyd-Jones who said, "The problem is that when these trials come we tend to see nothing but the trials."[13] In order to make it through our struggles we must see past them to the God behind them, and that takes an active pursuit of him.

Failure to turn to God leads to a downward spiral. Talking about the temptation to not press into God Sinclair Ferguson said, "Of course nothing is more tempting when we go through the blues than to neglect prayer and God's word, witnessing and worship. But nothing will more rapidly lead to increasing lethargy."[14] Proverbs says a crushed spirit will lead to ruin (Prov 17:22, 18:14), and the way to turn from ruin is to turn to the one who is unshaken by our trials. It is trusting in him who keeps our hearts secure. We don't know why such things have happened to us, but we know who can help us, and we turn to him.

We turn to God and we find a firm place to stand that keeps us from sinking into ruin. Psalm 46 says "God is our refuge and strength, an ever-present help in trouble" (v1) and even if "the earth give way" and "mountains fall into the heart of the sea" we will not fear (v2). The reason for the psalmist's hope is that his hope is in God's dwelling place, which will never fall (v4-5). Because of this hope he can "be still" (v10) even in difficulties. In God we find an anchor for our soul that keeps us from being drug away by the turbulent tides of life.

In contrast to the healing effect of God's word, Martin Lloyd Jones said, "most of your unhappiness in life is due to the fact that you are listening to yourself instead of talking to yourself."[15] When we are focused on the trial we tend to dwell on

---

[12] Wingren 234.

[13] Martin Lloyd-Jones, *Spiritual Depression* (Grand Rapids: Eerdmans Publishing Company, 1965), 230.

[14] Sinclair Ferguson, *The Christian Life* (Carlisle, PA: Banner of Truth Trust, 1981), 180.

[15] Lloyd-Jones, 20.

it, convince ourselves how hopeless our situation is, and even conceive an imaginary situation far worse than reality. Speaking scripture to ourselves rather than listening to our own complaints can lift us out of self-pity and fill us with faith and hope.

God's truth provided a turning point for David in his difficult season. In these times he turned to God in open and honest confession saying, "Will you forget me forever? How long will you hide your face from me? How long must I wrestle with my thoughts and every day have sorrow in my heart?" (Psalm 13:1-2). Yet David did not remain in this place. He turned confidently to the one who could deliver him, so that later in the same psalm he could say "But I trust in your unfailing love; my heart rejoices in your salvation. I will sing to the LORD, for he has been good to me" (Psalm 13:5-6). David trusted in the unfailing love of God, and this led him to sing. He had profound hope that transcended and transformed his circumstances.

It is important to press into God to anchor our souls and to gain direction for the future. Many people who fail to turn to God in disappointments end up doing things contrary to his ways. They look for an easy way out, they lie to get a better job, or disregard commitments, and such weak-willed people only make their situation worse. We must press into God for strength because difficult decisions will need to be made, and we need God's direction for these. Should I fold the business, take a new job, or keep pressing on in the current situations? These are difficult situations that involve hard decisions, and necessitate pressing into him more than ever.

6.3 Have You Missed Your Calling?

We have covered the main points for persevering through difficulties, but touching on a few other topics is still necessary. One of these is addressing questions on calling. Times of disappointment will cause us to question God's purposes like few other things do. We will wonder if we made a bad decision, took the wrong job, or outright missed the will of God. A wrong understanding of calling can exacerbate our struggles, and for this reason we explore the finality and clarity of calling.

People have misunderstood the finality of a calling by thinking that since God called them to a particular job they should never leave it. This view of calling becomes very problematic when we are in a job situation we don't want to be in. It leads us to think we can never leave. This view of calling has been popular in the past, but it simply is not biblical. Just because God calls us to one job does not mean we shouldn't press on towards another. David herded sheep for a season and then reigned as king. Moses did the same. Amos was a shepherd then a prophet (Amos 7:14, 15). James and John were fishermen and then apostles. God does not call a person irrevocably to a particular job. His calling comes in the form of specific tasks for specific seasons and not as a once for all-time placement. There are seasons where we may work at one job and seasons we move to another.

This should encourage those who are in a position they don't want to be in. Just because you are there now does not mean it is forever. And as unmarried person makes much effort pursuing a spouse, so also it is appropriate to give much effort to pursuing the career you desire to be in. In seasons of vocational disappointment we must not lose sight of where we would like to be. We acknowledge God has us where we are, but then press on to where we would like to be in hopes that he may open another opportunity.

A second way people struggle with a "missed calling" is by expecting some kind of spectacular confirmation or sign from God about which job to take. Paul saw Jesus on the Damascus road. Isaiah was commissioned with a powerful vision. David had a prophet anoint him. Joseph had dreams. Contrary to these, I simply had an overweight middle aged man with glasses tell me he could use some help. The instances of those who had miraculous experiences can often lead others with less miraculous experiences to doubt they even have a calling, or if they are where God intends.

The miraculous calling of people should be seen as expressions of God's grace to give that particular person confidence in what God was calling them to do. People today may experience this in differing degrees, and some may find more clarity in their calling than others. I know quite a few people who through various events have great confidence and fascinating stories of how they were directed to their jobs. That is God's grace to them, but that is not my experience, nor the majority of other people. Many can relate to people like Luke, who wrote his gospel because it seemed like a good idea (Luke 1:3). In most cases there will not be supernatural experiences giving assurance for what to do. If your only confirmation for taking a job is that you needed a job, this one "seemed good," and they hired you, then you should be confident that God frequently works in this way.

It is the grace of God that gives some people very obvious direction in their calling, but such miraculous callings are not the norm and should not be the standard we put on determining calling. Most of us will not have such assurance and clarity, and will instead have some mystery in discovering our calling for the right job. In speaking of the mystery of calling Os Guinness said,

> Can you state your identity in a single sentence? No more should you necessarily be able to state your calling in a single sentence. At best you can only specify a part of it. And even that clarity may have to be qualified. In many cases a clear sense of calling comes only through a time of searching, including trial, and error.[16]

We live life by faith, and that faith will be required in the jobs we take. There is no guarantee we will have spectacular confirmation for where to work, but that should not discourage us. As we pursue our callings, there may be times it feels like taking a job is a trial and error process or that we are just doing "what seems good," but God often uses such things to lead us, and behind these things may very well be the hidden hand of God.

6.4 Discipline or Disappointment?

In times of hardship sometimes the question is asked, "Is God disciplining me?" In other words have you committed some sin that resulted in God bringing this difficulty upon you? This is a legitimate question, because just as our earthly fathers discipline us, so also God disciplines those he loves (Heb 12:6).

---

[16] Guinness, 51.

Every situation we encounter should be approached with the attitude of "What might God be showing me in this?" and the question is relevant in difficulties too. Sometimes there may be a pattern of sin that God is addressing by bringing difficulty on us. I have seen people encounter a difficulty and immediately connect it to a clear and obvious wrong doing. They misled customers and were soon losing business and fearing confrontation. When hardship comes, and we see a clear connection between the hardship and a sin, we need to confess our sins, turn to Christ. When this happens following Christ may involve digging ourselves out of a deep whole by doing hard things in the right way.

But not all hardship should be associated with God's discipline. The hardship we are encountering may very well be the difficulties of life under the curse, and in that case we may do harm in trying to "find the sin" that is causing our difficulties. When it is the difficulties of life we are encountering the solution is to press on and not give up.

If we are uncertain about our difficulty being the result of discipline or difficulty it is a good idea to share your hardships, as well as what you think may be the cause of them, with a pastor or spiritually mature friend. Outside perspective can be extremely helpful in determining if there was sin, whether or not the sin and trial are related, and how to potentially deal with the situation and its consequences. This requires openness and honesty, but it could be the means by which we discern whether the situation requires repentance and faith or hard work and diligence.

6.5 Evaluate with Sober Judgment

Another culprit of disappointment is having expectations that are not realistic. Overestimating our gifting and abilities can cause chronic disappointment. We have major league aspirations but minor league skills. We think we deserve the big time salary, the head job, or the influential role and are disappointed when it does not come. In speaking of the tendency for people to think too highly of their position in life Martin Luther said, "It is possible to estimate one's proper station in such a way that a whole kingdom would not suffice."[17]

It is not hard to find instances of this in life. Right now television is filled with talent shows that allow people to audition for big time contracts, and it is amazing to see people who are so bad and yet so determined they have the talent to make the big time. They have a misguided perception of their gifts and abilities. They are disappointed because their pride has led them to think too highly of themselves. They need a good friend to speak some hard love into their lives (Prov 27:6). There is a clear lack of gifting, but they fail to see it because of their pride.

Romans 12:3 tells us to evaluate ourselves with sober judgment and not think too highly of ourselves. It means we evaluate ourselves soberly and maybe even with the help of sober-minded friends or sober-minded bosses and coworkers. We ask them what we can grow in, and if our goals and dreams are worth pursuing in the near or distant future. This keeps us from seeking a stage in life that is beyond our gifting.

Asking questions about our abilities also puts us in position to learn and grow. It is a long hard road to gaining a successful career, and getting advice from close friends will help us know which battles we should fight for and which we should not. I have often found it extremely encouraging when pursuing something to ask my wife, family, or friends what they think about what I am doing. Their thoughts are not determinative, but they always lead to making better judgments. Not assuming we already have what it takes to do what we want to do is key to growing into what we want to become.

Lastly, the gospel helps us to evaluate ourselves soberly and leads to true hope in our weakness and limitation. We must guard against thinking too highly of ourselves or hoping in our work, because it is certain that one day our work will fail us. One day our work will not be able to sustain our life, and we need to trust the one whose work will sustain us. That is Jesus Christ, whose work was to live a sinless life, die on the cross, and ascend to the right hand of God. His work is the work we hope in and

---

[17] Martin Luther, "Address to the Nobility of the German Nation," point 22 in *Luther Works*, vol 44.

what will provide everlasting life. We are not the Savior, and our work will fail. His work is what we look to and put our hope in, and this leads to viewing our work with appropriate sobriety.

6.6 A Story to Close With

As we close this chapter on disappointment, I want to share an inspiring story of a friend who encountered disappointments in the right way. Mark went to college to play football at a big time program. He was highly recruited out of high school and had a promising future, but after arriving at a school with a lot of talented guys, he did not have the success he hoped to have. He was gifted and dedicated, but the competition was great, and he was not finding opportunity on the football field.

During this disappointing season he contemplated transferring to a smaller school to get more playing time, but decided against it. He knew his current school provided a better opportunity to make it to the NFL, which was his goal. One day he read through the story of Joseph and found much encouragement with Joseph being faithful even in a dungeon. He decided to focus on glorifying God by trusting God for opportunity and being faithful with what he could do. For two years his work ethic gained the respect of his coaches and other players, but he still sat on the bench, only occasionally going in to block on kickoffs and special teams.

It was during the biggest rivalry game of Mark's junior year that he once again lined up to block on a kickoff return, but something unexpected happened this time. The opposing team's kicker shanked the kick, and instead of the ball going deep to the end zone, it was a waffling short kick that landed (sovereignly) in Mark's hands. After working faithfully for two years, Mark knew exactly what to do and he was ready for it. He caught the ball and took off running. With a couple nifty moves he ran 89 yards for a touchdown and the stadium erupted in cheers.

This was the turning point in Mark's career. It was an opportunity for him to show what he could do, and it was made possible through years of faithfulness in little things. He kept the faith in hard times, sought to grow and get better each day, and so he was ready when God opened an opportunity. The following year Mark would be a starter on offense, defense, and special teams, and he would go on to have a good career in the NFL. If he had not persevered through his disappointments he never would have met his goal. In the disappointing times Mark focused on the ultimate goal, trusted God, was faithful with small things, and pressed in to God. He made the most of this time and it opened opportunities that ended his disappointing season.

Chapter 6 Discussion Questions

1. What is your greatest source of disappointment in your current job? How does this chapter change your perspective on that disappointment?

2. How does the experience of biblical characters inform your understanding of suffering and how to press through it?

3. How does the chief goal of glorifying God inform and temper your disappointments?

4. In your work what do you need to be faithful with and what do you need to trust God with?

5. What truths of scripture are most encouraging to you and which truths do you most struggle to believe in this season?

Chapter 7

Idolatry—When Work Serves the Wrong Master

"I am the LORD your God, who brought you out of Egypt, out of the land of slavery. You shall have no other gods before me. You shall not make for yourself an idol in the form of anything in heaven above or on the earth beneath or in the waters below. You shall not bow down to them or worship them; for I, the LORD your God, am a jealous God,"
Exodus 20:2-5

Seeing the word "idolatry" in the chapter title of a book on work may seem out of place. After all, when we think of "idols" it brings to mind stone statues or totem poles that some primitive tribe would dance and celebrate around. Idolatry doesn't seem relevant to our lives, much less to our work, but there is a sobering connection.

The foundations for understanding idolatry are laid in the Old Testament, and yes, in some ways it could be described as primitive, yet the implications are staggeringly relevant. Idolatry in the Old Testament centered on worshiping hand crafted images that resembled an alleged god. An idol was basically a material object representing a deity, and as it represented the deity, worshipping the idol was considered worshipping the god it represented.

The idol that gave the Israelites the most temptation was named Baal, and the people's worship of this idol seems to have revolved around preserving their livelihood. The ancient Israelites did not do business over the internet nor were they interested in updating their websites. They were an agricultural nation interested in producing crops. They lived off the land, and their survival and prosperity was dependent on the productivity of that land. If the land produced much then business and life were good. If it was a dry year where crops withered and died, then so would they.

Water was essential for their crops to grow, and the main problem for the Israelites was that the major rivers and lakes were lower than the land. This meant they couldn't irrigate their crops from nearby water sources. In order to have a great harvest they were completely dependent on rain to water their fields. There was little in their control, and they had to depend on God to provide rain (Deut 11:10-17).

This is where Baal comes in. Baal was the god of the Canaanites—the other people in the land. He was known as the Storm God, and the one they claimed the land depended on for the rain. The Canaanites believed Baal controlled the rain and would bring it only if he was worshipped sufficiently. Worshipping Baal posed a serious temptation for Israelites hoping to secure their fortunes.

Worshiping Baal, or any other idol, was a serious offense to God and went against the very first commandment of God: "You shall have no other gods before me" (Ex 20:3). Turning to worship Baal was in fact turning away from God. As soon as their allegiance to God shifted, the door to a host of evils was opened. Worshippers of Baal were known to cut their bodies with knives and indulge in sexual immorality and prostitution at temples. Some idol worship even involved sacrificing children. All this was done in hopes of pleasing him, so he would bring rains and an abundant harvest.

Worship of Baal was seen in many ways. Some abandoned God completely to worship Baal, but the most dominant was mixing the worship of Baal with the worship of God. People would worship God, but they may also visit temples of Baal. They would worship God but also cut their bodies. It was a blended worship as if they were trying to cover all their bases.

They failed to see that the worship of idols, even in small degrees, was a rejection of God, and the rejection of the single-hearted devotion God called them to (Deut 6:4-5). They were abandoning the true God and turning to lifeless things and detestable practices, all for the sake of ensuring their fortunes. The actions of their idolatry showed that God was not the one their trust and confidence was in.

The reasons for their idolatry are manifold but ultimately centered on a lack of trust in God. They did not trust God fully and found it acceptable to justify doing things God had forbidden. Since they did not trust God, they turned in dependence on other things. They put their trust in their own ability to secure their fortunes. They worked how they thought best and not as God dictated. Acquiring a great crop was more important than worshipping God, and they would do whatever it took to acquire a harvest, even if it meant bowing to another god. Through their unbelief and idolatry they dethroned God and enthroned another master.

Eugene Merril said their idolatry was, "turning from God, the real source of prosperity and fertility, to the figment of depraved imaginations. It was in every way an egregious act of covenant rebellion and disloyalty."[1] Their idolatry was foolish and appalling, but we should remember it is no different than when we trust things other than God for our sustenance, survival, and security. No matter how foolish and primitive their worship of idols appeared, it is just as outrageous when we choose to worship and trust in anything other than God. Like the Israelites, we too will face many temptations to turn from the living God and serve other masters in hopes of securing a harvest.

7.1 Idolatry in Today's World

Baal is gone today and what is left are only ancient artifacts to remind of his ultimate failure, yet the nature of people to trust in things other than the true God is clearly present. We are just as prone to worship fabricated gods as people were four thousand years ago. Not only is it true today, but in the history of the world there has been "no period in which people were free from the attraction of idols."[2] While the objects of what we worship may have changed, the tendency to put our trust in something other than God remains.

---

[1] Eugene Merrril, *Kingdom of Priests* (Grand Rapids: Baker Books, 1987), 161.

[2] F. B. Huey, Jr, "Idolatry," in vol 3 of *The Zondervan Pictoral Encyclopedia of the Bible,* edited by Merrill C. Tenney (Grand Rapids: Zondervan, 1976), 245.

127

The New Testament shows a shift from idolatry involving the worship of graven images to anything that may detract, divert, or negate God of the glory and worship that he alone deserves. Martin Luther said, "Whatever your heart clings to and relies upon, that is your God; trust and faith of the heart alone make both God and idol."[3] An idol is anything apart from God that we attach hope to and put confidence in.

When our security and hope are attached to work our heart will cling to it for survival. We think work rather than God is the true sustainer of our lives, and we will live for it rather than God. If our hope is in work, we will give ourselves to serving it. It becomes our identity, and as our work goes so we go.

When we become idolaters we are willing to rearrange our lives to serve the idol. We will do whatever it takes to gain or please that idol. When our hope is in money we will sacrifice ourselves, bodies, even children in hopes of gaining it. In a time when families are divided, parents neglect children, and people are constantly taken advantage of when buying and selling, and all in an allegedly "Christian" nation, it does not take long to realize the worship of God is being compromised.

Idolatry isn't always as easy to find as simply asking someone who their God is. Since idolatry involves the heart, it can be very subtle. Idolatry can most often be seen in what functionally drives us. It is what we practically gear our life around. We do not label it formally as a "God" and bow down to it, but it is what our life is focused on and what our decisions are based on. We may confess to worship the living God, but in reality our worship has been blended with worship of an idol. We have abandoned the exclusive worship of God.

Our idol is what we spend time pursuing, what is most valued and most revered. Money certainly is a common idol, but it could just as well be the opinion of others. We crave approval and praise from others, and we labor for that. We work with our head to the ground with no regard to anything else, and everything revolves around looking and being successful. We yearn to hear others speak highly of us. We work to please our boss and give little to no thought how we might serve God. Our desire to gain

---

[3] Martin Luther, *Larger Catechism,* "The First Commandment."

this idol causes us to put other God given responsibilities aside—even family and friends. Our work is not labeled as a God, but it clearly has the highest priority in life. It is where our true hope and security lay, and we are willing to abandon God to ensure our fortunes in the office.

Idolatry does not always involve desiring something evil. Often idolatry comes when we desire something good, but we desire it too strongly.[4] David Powlison said, "The evil in our desire often lies not in what we want but in the fact that we want it too much."[5] It is not wrong to desire to be a successful business person, but when that desire becomes too great it can become a controlling idol. We reorder our lives around that master.

Inordinate desires are usually associated with greed and covetousness (Col 3:5, Eph 5:5), and as there is no lack of objects for people to covet, there is no lack of potential idols. It could be money, fame, prestige, possessions, houses, friends, and vacations. It is anything that diverts us from trusting and serving God. People are so prone to elevate good things to supreme importance that it led John Calvin to say "man's nature is a perpetual factory of idols."[6] As a factory produces goods so our hearts produce idols. Always finding something tangible to put our hope and trust in. Idols roll out of our hearts like cars off an assembly line.

Every day at the office temptation abounds: the temptation to worship our income, promotions, possessions, approval of others, and the list goes on and on. When an idol like one of these arises, our work will serve a master other than God. Work can either be the idol or the primary means of worshiping the idol. When this happens it means we are no longer working for true lasting glory, but rather a fool's gold that will soon perish.

---

[4] John Calvin, *Institutes,* 3.3.12.
[5] David Powlison, *Seeing With New Eyes* (Phillipsburg: P&R Publishing, 2003), 149. Powlison effectively summarizes Calvin with this statement.
[6] Calvin, *Institutes,* 1.11.8.

7.2 Consequences of Idolatry: The Danger of Getting What You Want

Idolatry is taking the glory and honor that God alone deserves and giving it to something else. It is trading the glory of the immortal God for created things (Rom 1:23), and it distorts the very purpose we were created for. Brian Rosner said idolatry is, "The ultimate expression of unfaithfulness to God and for that reason the occasion for severe divine punishment."[7] Anytime we reject the authority of those that stand over us there are severe consequences, and this is true of God as well.

Idolatry is an expression of serious unfaithfulness, and therefore it has serious consequences. Chris Wright said, "To refuse to glorify God, and even worse, 'to exchange the glory of the immortal God for images made to look like mortal man and birds and animals and reptiles' (Rom 1:23) is to frustrate the purpose of our very existence. Idolatry is radical self-harm."[8] When we commit idolatry we are destroying ourselves.

The only thing certain with idolatry is that it will one day let us down. Idols cannot save us nor protect us, so when we put our trust in them a frequent consequence is being let down by them. A friend of mine was a very hard and successful worker with serious skills, but one day his company decided to make some difficult cuts, and he was one of them. He was devastated by being let go, and it took months for him to recover. It was extremely painful, because he never thought of himself as expendable. The perfect image he had of himself was destroyed, and it was very humbling, but as he began to come out of his disappointment he realized he had put his trust in the wrong thing. He put his hope in his abilities and was feeling the effects of living with hope in something destined to fail.

Having an idol taken away is painful, but it is not the only form of punishment. When people forsake God and refuse to

---

[7] B.S. Rosner, "Idolatry," in *New Dictionary of Biblical Theology*, T. Desmond Alexander, Brian S. Rosner, D.A. Carson and Graeme Goldsworthy editors (Downers Grove: InterVarsity Press, 2000), 570.

[8] Christopher Wright, *Mission of God* (Downers Grove: InterVarsity Press, 2006), 172.

glorify him as God, he sometimes vindicates his glory by giving people over to their darkened desires (Rom 1:24). This giving them over to their desires can be part of the punishment. Psalm 115 shows this connection between idol worship and its punishment. The psalm first speaks of idols and then ends with a powerful conclusion about those who worship them saying,

> But their idols are silver and gold, made by the hands of men. They have mouths, but cannot speak, eyes, but they cannot see; they have ears, but cannot hear, noses, but they cannot smell; they have hands, but cannot feel, feet, but they cannot walk; nor can they utter a sound with their throats. Those who make them will be like them, and so will all who trust in them. (Psa 115:4-8)

The idols of people are lifeless. They are dead, insensitive, cold, unfeeling, and impotent. Though they have ears they cannot hear, and though they have mouths they cannot speak. In the end it is madness to worship them, but the most surprising and sobering verse, is that those who make them become like them. One main consequence of idolatry is that "we become like what we worship."[9]

The relation of idolatry and punishment is made even clearer in the book of Isaiah. Isaiah brought a message of judgment to the people of Israel who were steeped in idolatry. God tells Isaiah to go to this people saying, "Be ever hearing but never understanding; ever seeing but never perceiving. Make the heart of this people calloused; make their ears dull and close their eyes" (Isaiah 6:9-10). The conclusion of this is that idolatrous Israel is now deaf, blind, heartless, and cold; in effect they have become like the lifeless objects they worshipped.

We become like what we worship. Earthly things are lifeless, and we become lifeless like them: cold, blind, insensitive and unfeeling. Unaffected by the joys of life, idolaters stand motionless and unmoved—simply craving for more of what will

---

[9] G. K. Beal, *We Become What we Worship* (Downers Grove: Inter-Varsity Press, 2008).

never fulfill them. They are never satisfied and are equally unaffected by the wrong they do to others to satisfy their gods.

In Romans 1 when people turn from the living God, he gives them over to a depraved mind. They are filled and inflamed with every kind of wickedness and become among other things arrogant, faithless, heartless, ruthless, and deceitful. The fruit of idolatry is part of the punishment of idolatry. Whether it is a lifeless idol of a graven image of Baal, the graven image of money, or a self conceived trophy for being the world's greatest _____ (you fill in the blank) the result of idolatry is the same—lifelessness.

We take on the qualities of what we worship to some degree or another. 2 Kings 17:15 says, the people "followed worthless idols and themselves became worthless." If we worship worthless or shameful things then we become like them. The punishment of giving God's glory to another is that we are destroyed by what we worship.

Chris Wright said, "When people worship creation instead of the creator, everything is turned upside down. Idolatry produces disorder in all our fundamental relationships."[10] The worship of God is for his glory and *our* good, and the neglect of worshiping him is to our detriment. "We resemble what we revere, either for ruin or restoration."[11] If we revere God, the giver of life who is holy, good, gracious, truthful, and righteous then we will become like him, but when we revere dead and lifeless things, we also become dead and lifeless.

A sobering example of such ruin is seen in Carl and Vicky. They were a married couple who started an insurance company together hoping to acquire a nice and comfortable life. They focused intensely on the company, and it slowly became profitable, and soon they began pushing to make it to the next level. Eventually they were able to buy a bigger house and nicer cars, and so they pushed harder and harder to prosper the business. They soon fixed their eyes on a new boat, an even bigger house, and a more and more posh lifestyle.

---

[10] Wright, *Mission of God,* 143.

[11] G. K. Beal, *We Become What we Worship* (Downers Grove: Inter-Varsity Press, 2008), 49.

The success of the business slowly consumed them. Their lives were squarely centered on making more money. As their earnings became greater so did their expectations. They were never satisfied, and the result was a debilitating obsession with money and possessions. Everything they did was done with the intent of achieving greater gain for greater vacations, better cars, bigger houses, and a more and more luxurious life. The business was prospering greatly, but they were not satisfied.

Carl soon found himself consumed with watching the rise and fall of his stocks. No matter how much he watched they never seemed to rise high enough, and when they fell he was he fell too. His hope and identity were tied to these idols, and they were destroying him. He developed an obsession for his work and a volatile tempter that fluctuated with his perceived prosperity.

Carl and Vicky had pushed aside most of their family and friendships to work on the business. They viewed their children as a hindrance to their work. They rarely saw them, and even when they did they were preoccupied with work. Carl and Vicky even began treating each other terribly. When they had a bad day they took out their frustration in cold and heartless actions on each other. They grew numb to gentle jabs and soon began ignoring, shoving, and yelling at each other.

Ironically they had more than they ever dreamed of, but they were emptier than they could ever have imagined. They were worshiping the god of money, and they had become as cold, unfeeling, and heartless as the very thing they worshiped. They were becoming like their god, and it was destroying them. Their idolatry was indeed radical self-harm.

Many will find themselves at the height of a career and at the top of their profession only to look around and see no one beside them. The danger of idolatry is sacrificing everything to that idol, to our own detriment. This is where I too am sobered at how easily we can destroy ourselves running after careers. As I type these words, my four year old son and two year old daughter are running around me. There are times I would like nothing better than to lock myself in a quiet room for months and get this book written. It sobers me to think how easily time could go by and I have a great career, but have sacrificed these precious children for it.

It is a tragedy to go through life sacrificing the most precious and enriching parts of life to idols, and it is an even greater tragedy to sacrifice the living God for our idols. Idolaters choose to fulfill their own lusts rather than be with God, and this great tragedy becomes the greatest punishment. Idolaters desire life apart from God and they get it—to their own detriment.

The greatest punishment is the complete loss of God—eternity without him. God essentially says, "You did not want to spend your life in fellowship with me and my people on this earth. All right, I will give you what you wanted on this earth for eternity: separation from God and his people."[12] It is a scary thing to push God from our lives, because life without God interfering is hell, and this is what idolatry leads to.

Idolatry is a vicious cycle of creating an idol, worshipping it, and becoming like it. Stopping this cycle begins with identifying our idols, but it does not stop there. Tim Keller said "The only way to free ourselves from the destructive influence of counterfeit gods is to turn back to the true one."[13] If we wish to free ourselves from idolatry and its consequences we must turn completely to the living God. And the good news of the gospel is that when we turn to the living God we can be forgiven for our sin and also transformed to his likeness with ever increasing glory (2 Cor 3:18). Through Christ we can be forgiven for our idolatry and can regain what was lost.

7.3 A Servant of One Master

To free ourselves from idols and work for true glory, we must worship God alone. As soon as an idol appears in our lives it begins to drive a wedge between us and God. Having an idol is like bringing along an old flame on a date with your spouse. It causes immediate problems. When an idol is present one will be unable to give God the single-hearted devotion he commands. An idol's demands always contradict the demands of God. When our idol is money, and we attach our security to it, then we justify all kinds of

---

[12] Beal, 47.
[13] Tim Keller, *Counterfeit Gods* (Dutton: New York, 2009), xxiv.

things to acquire it. It will cause us to act differently than God commands, and a crack in our devotion soon becomes a gaping hole. For this reason it was said "Idolatry is the beginning, cause, and end of every evil" (Wis 14:27). This is why it is important to have only one master.

Matthew 6:24 says, "No one can serve two masters. Either he will hate the one and love the other, or he will be devoted to the one and despise the other. You cannot serve both God and Money." It is impossible to be devoted to money or any other idol and still serve God. Two masters always have conflicting demands for their subjects. Their service takes on two completely different paths and leads to two completely different places.

It is like a man who takes on two jobs, and not just any jobs but two demanding jobs. At some point the two will interfere with each other. One will need him when he is with the other. He may be working diligently on a deadline, trying to make sure that every detail is in place for a presentation, when inevitably, the phone rings. It is his other boss, the other master, calling for his attention. He is unable to give his complete attention and service to the project, and it gets left undone. He has to choose which master is most important, and which he is going to serve.

Many head to the office in the morning to do much good for God's kingdom when their other boss starts calling. He has another agenda, and it does not involve God's plan. As we scan the horizons of our lives to see what our hope and trust are in, there should be one figure and one figure alone whose prominence rises far above all others. So prominently that everything else is seen in relation to that one figure. This is the place of God.

It is God that must be our true master and the one we are most passionate about. Often we falsely think that by not hating God we are somehow serving him. But here again idolatry is much more subtle than we typically think. When two masters are present we may love one and hate the other, or it may be that we are interested in one and not interested in the other. Disinterest can be the most deceiving form of idolatry. We say that we are "just not as into God as others" or "work is more fun than church." This is saying we are interested in God only as long as it doesn't interfere with our other bosses. Our disinterest makes God a second rate master who only gets the leftovers.

Disinterest in God is the result of serving another master. Any time there are rival masters in the mix it means we are not serving our true master, and we are no better than Canaanites who foolishly worshipped wooden images on their way to the temple of God. We are called to worship God alone without any intrusions, and false worship needs to be dealt with decisively.

In the Middle Ages there was a missionary to Germany named Boniface. There is a famous story of him encountering a tribal people who worshipped idols and magic. The center of this people's idolatry was a sacred oak tree dedicated to their alleged "Thundergod." Appalled by their idolatry Boniface was convinced drastic measures needed to be taken. One day he assembled all the people at this sacred oak tree, picked up his axe, took off his shirt, and with everyone looking on he began to chop the tree down. They were shocked by his acts, but with their tree lying on the ground and Boniface standing next to it, they realized how futile their god was. Their idol couldn't even protect itself! Boniface took drastic measures to hack down idols, and we should do the same with ourselves.

We need to put to death our idols (Col 3:5). Part of chopping down our idols is cultivating faith and trust in the true God. Worshiping God with single-hearted devotion requires recognizing that he alone deserves to be worshiped. He alone is eternal, he alone is sovereign, he alone sees everything, he alone gives life, he alone provides for all our needs.

When we see him for what he is we see that he alone is worthy to be worshipped, and he alone is greater than our detestable idols. His ways lead to true life and knowing this will lead us to worship him passionately in our work. Seeing his greatness will lead to serving him and being transformed into his image. When we struggle to see him as such we should pray with Augustine that God would, "become sweet to me beyond all the allurements that I used to follow."[14] We need to ask God to open our cold hearts and blind eyes so we can see him as he actually is, better than anything the world offers. This leads to becoming a servant of one master.

---

[14] Augustine, *Confessions* (Nashville: Thomas Nelson Publishers, 1999), 17.

7.4 Working Like God Really is the Boss

What we believe affects how we act. The master we serve determines how we live. If God is worshiped in life it will lead to a holy ethic where our actions, decisions, and life reflect the God we serve. If we worship idols it will promote a distinctly different ethic. Christopher Wright said, "Idolatry always has disastrous social and ethical effects. How we behave depends on what or whom we worship."[15] Idolatry is often seen in the adverse effects it has on others.

God calls us to love our neighbor (Matt 22:37-39) and to do to them as we want them to do to us (Luke 6:31), but idolatry subverts God's rule and leads us to take advantage of our neighbors. When work becomes an idol people will say and do all kinds of things to others. Common phrases used to justify their terrible actions include, "The end justifies the means," "Might makes right," "Do whatever it takes to get what you want," and "As long as you are happy." These sayings attempt to vindicate selfish pursuits of our own kingdom and fail to take into account that God is very interested in *how* we achieve success.

Many want success, but few are willing to achieve it in the manner God commands. Many want God to bless them, but not in the manner he offers. We must resist compromising to the evil ways of the world. The ethic we work with should show God is the one we love and serve. If we love God we will obey his commands (John 14:21) and work in the way he calls us to. We are not content to acquire wealth, money, or power in just any manner but rather in a manner that pleases God and does good to others. When we work in a way that destroys other people it shows God is not the one we serve.

Our lives should reflect an ultimate and uncompromising allegiance to God and others. The greatest example of such allegiance in the face of temptation is in Jesus' resistance of Satan's temptation. Matthew 4:8-9 says, "Again, the devil took him to a very high mountain and showed him all the kingdoms of

---

[15] Christopher Wright, *Old Testament Ethics and the People of God* (Downers Grove: Intervarsity Press, 2004), 25.

the world and their splendor. 'All this I will give you,' he said, 'if you will bow down and worship me.'"

Jesus is tempted with great prosperity and glory through a means that would subvert the Father's will. It is a temptation to great renown and great earthly glory. It is not just one kingdom offered but all. And it would be his immediately with very little hardship or difficulty. It was fame and splendor, and it would come with no more work than a bowing of the knee and a few words of allegiance. John MacArthur says, "Satan offers what seems to be the same as what God offers, but his price is much cheaper."[16]

Satan's temptation is for Jesus to break the first commandment, not through a doctrinal statement or written belief, but through an action, a step of building his kingdom. It was a temptation to success and great glory that would come through a simple, yet earth shattering bowing of the knee. The temptation here is to go about his mission not in the manner God desired, but in a much easier manner.

It was a great temptation to acquire his kingdom not through hard work and painful sacrifice—the way of the cross, but through a simple means of denying God and worshipping another. It was a temptation that people sell themselves to everyday for so, so, so much less than what Christ was offered.

Everyday people are challenged to compromise their mission by the success syndrome and empire building. They find an easier way to build their kingdom. They look away from questionable practices and give in when it is advantageous.[17] False promises and lies are spoken to customers. Coworkers turn on each other to get a leg up on the other. Justice is traded for profit. Women prostitute themselves with skimpy clothes to gain favor. Kingdoms are no doubt being built but at the cost of selling their soul to the devil.

One of the greatest signs of idolatry and compromise today is the willingness to hurt or tempt others in efforts to build our kingdom. If God is our true master we must be content to gain things in the manner he desires, and our trust in him should lead us to do things that are good for others.

---

[16] John MacArthur, *Matthew 1-7,* (Chicago: Moody Press, 1985), 97.
[17] Ibid

One of the most helpful and revealing pieces of advice I have ever received about doing business in a manner that glorifies God came from a beloved professor who was teaching on the book of Proverbs. He said that in Proverbs "The righteous are willing to disadvantage themselves in order to advantage others, and the wicked are willing to disadvantage others in order to advantage themselves."[18] Idolaters are willing to hurt others to further their own good, but the righteous put others above themselves.

This sets a God-honoring bar for our actions, and I have found this a helpful litmus test for my intentions. In times when the line seems fuzzy and confusing asking the questions of who is being put at a disadvantage and who is being put at an advantage can be extremely revealing. It helps determine if we are really working for the good of others or just for ourselves, and if our work is really serving God or our idols. It puts God's glory and the good of others at the crux of our work. In many ways it connects the golden rule ("Do to others as you would have them do to you." Luke 6:31) to our work in a fresh way, and shows the right way to work.

When God is our true master there is contentment in what he provides and commands. We would rather gain things his way or not gain them at all. We would rather go without something than gain it by hurting others. When we are content with God and what he has provided then we will work in a manner that honors him and betters others. This is when his laws become delightful boundaries (Psalm 16:6) that lead to working with a holy and life-giving ethic that honors God and does good to others.

7.5 Making the Right Sacrifice

We have made much about work throughout this book, and rightfully so, but there are many idolaters that give a hardy amen to such teaching. They agree on working diligently, with excellence, and for a greater influence, because they clothe their idolatry in a veil of godly piety. They sacrifice their lives to make more

---

[18] Bruce Waltke, *The Book of Proverbs*, vol 1 (Grand Rapids: William B. Eerdmans, 2004), 97.

money—all in the name of honoring God. If we are going to use work as a means to glorify God there is going to come a time when we have to make sacrifices.

It is not by us reigning powerfully over a great kingdom (or great office) that advances God's kingdom most significantly. That can happen, but God's kingdom most often expands through great sacrifice. If we are going to emulate God in our work it will have to be done by emulating his sacrifice. Loren Wilkinson said, "The deepest truth of the Old Story of Christian orthodoxy is that the divine nature is most fully seen not in lordly transcendence, but in the agony of incarnation and crucifixion."[19] If we are going to show the world the greatness of God it will require imitating his sacrifice, and this is a hard pill for idolaters to swallow.

The disciples celebrated the powerful miracles Jesus performed, but they were confounded when he began to talk about laying down his life. They were fine with calling fire down from heaven (Luke 9:54), but questioned the call to be servants (Luke 9:46-48). We too are often fine with advancing the kingdom through awards and promotions, but cringe at the thought of sacrifice. It is as Thomas A Kempis said, "Jesus has many who love his heavenly kingdom, but few who bear his cross."[20]

Ultimately advancing the Gospel comes through sacrifice and service, the type of sacrifice and service that idolatry will oppose. Jesus made it clear that it was through laying down his life that he would triumph over all, and he made it clear that the way to true greatness and true glory will be the same for his followers. If we want to be great we must lay down our lives for others. We must lay down our lives to serve others just as Jesus "did not come to be served, but to serve and give his life as a ransom for many" (Mark 10:45).

It will take a willingness to sacrifice if we are going to share the gospel at work. It will take sacrifice to speak out against the sinful actions of others. It will take sacrifice to give of our income. It takes sacrifice to define success by doing good rather than by profits alone. It will require sacrifice to take time from

---

[19] Loren Wilkinson in R.P. Stevens, *The Other Six Days*, 99.
[20] Thomas a` Kempis, *Imitation of Christ* (Nashville: Thomas Nelson Publishers, 1999), 48.

work to serve in our church and to be there for our wife and children. These all involve sacrificing earthly gain, but they are essential to experiencing fullness of life in Christ and gaining eternal glory.

The kind of sacrifices we make will vary. Some may choose to sacrifice by moving to a new city for a new opportunity to further their career. Some may be called to sacrifice a great career opportunity in order to serve in their church or to have more time with family. Some will sacrifice career advancement by boldly proclaiming the gospel; others may keep quiet for a time so they can advance to a position that allows them to exert God-honoring policy over an entire organization.

There are various kinds of sacrifices, and it will not always look the same for all people. Daniel's unwavering commitment and bold proclamation of faith in God caused him to stick out like a sore thumb (Dan 3). He risked his life to make a bold proclamation of faith. But there is also Ester, who at times seems to have assimilated far too closely with the world. Nevertheless, in time she was clearly willing to sacrifice and take great risks for the good of her people. God used both of these people to advance his kingdom, because they did sacrifice.

Different people will be called to different sacrifices, and there will be seasons where the sacrifices we make vary. There are times to assimilate and times to boldly resist, but in the end what matters is that we do sacrifice to the Lord. It is through self sacrifice that the kingdom of God advances most profoundly, and such sacrifices are to be made daily (Luke 9:23). Everyday should involve making some type of sacrifice to Christ, and when we are not willing to sacrifice to him the most pressing question to ask is, "What idols are we worshiping?"

Idolatry will pervert the true goal of work, and Cornelius Plantinga described this perversion as "the turning of loyalty, energy, and desire away from God and God's project in the world: it is the diversion of construction materials for the city of God to side projects of our own."[21] We must see that the call to sacrifice for the kingdom of God will be opposed by the desire to build our

---

[21] Cornelius Plantiga, *Breviary of Sin* (Grand Rapids: William B. Eerdmans, 1995), 40.

own kingdom. If we are in the world to expand God's kingdom, then we need to evaluate how we may give of ourselves and resources to further his kingdom. We will not take our kingdoms with us to heaven, and so we should give our kingdoms to further his kingdom.

Conclusion

We all know the pain of a bad deal or an investment that goes south. People may place their lifesavings in stocks or real estate investments that seemed like a sure thing only to be left with nothing. It's painful and devastating, and yet this is ultimately what idolatry is. It is placing our whole life and being on an investment destined for failure. It is trading the infinite and eternal glory of God for things that will soon perish. Idolatry not only robs of true life in this world, but it also robs of eternal life. It is a serious sin, and one that must be fought against and destroyed if we are going to serve God.

Jesus is the only person who has fully succeeded in resisting the idolatrous temptation of the devil. He resisted that temptation to the point of shedding his blood and dying on the cross. He gave his life to rescue idolaters from the devastating effects of their sin, and he now offers new life to those who turn to him. His blood is for you, and it is by turning to him in faith that we can be saved from the detestable ways and disastrous effects of idolatry. Knowing and understanding his atoning death and the kingdom that it brings us into will lead to trust him fully and completely. Nothing else could do for us what he has accomplished through his life and death, and it is for that reason we must serve him alone as Lord of our life. He alone brings life, and therefore he alone is the one we worship, serve, and sacrifice to.

Chapter 7 Discussion Questions

1. Where are you most tempted to compromise your devotion to God in the work place?

2. Since idolatry can be so subtle, what areas do you need to be on guard against?

3. When you are worshipping idols and not God what are the consequences to those around you and to yourself?

4. What sacrifices is God calling you to make for him in your work? How can you do this on a daily basis?

Chapter 8

Shrewd as a Snake: Getting the Job Done in a Cruel World

"I am sending you out like sheep among wolves.
Therefore be as shrewd as snakes and as
innocent as doves."
Matthew 10:16

I had just started my first professional sales job. I had never before considered going into sales, and I was now wondering how to succeed in it. I thought hard work was important, but I also wanted to succeed in a manner that would glorify God. Since serving others is an important Christian practice, I decided the best way to succeed was to work hard at serving people, so that became my goal. I thought it was only a matter of time before the masses started flocking to me.

I experienced some early success with this approach, and after a few months I came in contact with my first potential large scale customer. I decided to go out of my way to serve them in hopes of winning them over, and of course, all for the glory of God! I did everything I could for them. Whatever they asked, I did it with great speed, joy, and pain staking precision—all done so they would have no doubts they were in good hands.

After weeks of working with them and countless hours spent on their account catering to their endless demands, my manager became interested in what was going on. He feared I was spending too much time with them and wanted to talk with the customer. At our meeting my manager gave an obligatory "Hey, how are you?" to the customer, and then he very abruptly (in his typical New Yorker style) cut straight to the chase. He asked the customer some very upfront questions that made me a little squeamish (he wasn't catering to their every need and that couldn't be serving them and winning them!). After asking simple but direct questions the customer wouldn't answer, my boss concluded an intrusive interrogation saying sternly, "If we do the things you are asking us, are you going to do business with us or are you wasting our time?" At that moment I was extremely perturbed and couldn't believe he would carelessly put my customer in this awkward position. Surely this was not the way to win their business!

It turned out his approach was not the way to win the deal, but it was the smart way to handle the situation. My manager was tipped off by a few things and suspected the customer was simply using me to get information in order to barter with his current vendor, which was exactly what was going on. He was in a contract and in no position to sign with me. He was letting me educate him on the product and then taking my color coded spreadsheets to his current vendor to work them over for a better deal. There was no way I was ever going to get his business, and I had foolishly wasted countless hours. I was taken advantage of, and that day I found out there was more to work than naively serving others.

I disagree with the harsh and uncaring attitude my manager approached the customer, but I commend him, because he suspected the customer was using me, so he asked smart direct questions that got to the heart of the situation. He used great wisdom in what he did, and this showed me I too needed to work wisely.

Many people enter into work like myself, focused on a few strengths or methods like serving and having a good attitude, but not aware of other important components necessary for working effectively. There are many challenges that confront us in work, and if we are going to overcome these and actually accomplish work that matters we will need to work with wisdom.

8.1 The Wisdom We Need

We will face many challenges in life, and these challenges make wisdom an absolute necessity. William Brakel explained the need for wisdom saying,

(Widsom) is an absolute necessity, for you are surrounded by your enemies, the devil is crafty, the world is deceptive, and the flesh tempts in a most subtle manner. You must either give up and let these enemies rule over you, or, if you wish to preserve your life, peace, and godliness you must be on guard prudently avoiding the snares which have been laid for you, and prudently carrying out that which the Lord has commanded you to do.[1]

We do not wish to give up or let our enemies rule over us. We want to succeed in work for the glory of God, and for that we must work wisely. We need wisdom for big sticky situations and for the small pesky things that daily confront us. Wisdom is essential for working effectively in the world and overcoming obstacles.

God has designed the world to function according to certain patterns, and wisdom helps us discern and live according to these patterns. Broadly speaking wisdom is "the practical knowledge of the laws of life and of the world."[2] It is knowing patterns like, "All hard work brings a profit" (Prov 14:23) and "Pride goes before destruction" (Prov 16:18). When we keep to the pattern of wisdom we will be blessed (Prov 8:32), protected, and rewarded (8:21). It is wisdom that helps us know how to successfully navigate the many precarious situations we inevitably find ourselves in.

To gain this wisdom we are going to look at characteristics that help us see God's intended patterns for the world. These characteristics of wisdom are given in the Bible, and in particular the book of Proverbs. It is here we gain insight into what it looks like to work wisely.

As we have many opponents in work, so also wisdom has many facets that will aid us. True wisdom is complex and not just a single feature. It involves an interworking of multiple characteristics: such as knowledge, insight, prudence, cunning,

---

[1] Wilhelmus a' Brakel, *Christian Reasonable Service*, vol 4, translated by Bartel Elshout, edited by Joel Beeke (Grand Rapids: Reformation Heritage Books, 1995), 135-6. Here Brakel speaks of prudence, which is virtually synonymous to wisdom.

[2] Gerhard von Rad, *Old Testament Theology*, translated by D.M.G. Stalker, Vol 1 (New York: Harper Row, 1962), 418.

discretion, learning, guidance, counsel, and strength. All these virtues come packaged with wisdom,[3] and their inter-relation is seen in passages like Proverbs 1:1-7

> The proverbs of Solomon son of David, king of Israel: for attaining wisdom and discipline; for understanding words of insight; for acquiring a disciplined and prudent life, doing what is right and just and fair; for giving prudence to the simple, knowledge and discretion to the young—let the wise listen and add to their learning, and let the discerning get guidance—for understanding proverbs and parables, the sayings and riddles of the wise. The fear of the LORD is the beginning of knowledge, but fools despise wisdom and discipline.

These many sides of wisdom function almost synonymously,[4] yet each one conveys a slightly different shade that colors our understanding. True wisdom contains all these various aspects, and working wisely requires each of their presence in some degree. We will now explore the aspects of skill, shrewdness, knowledge, prudence, diligence, and humility.

8.2 Skill

I struggled in my new job, because I lacked skill in it. My seasoned boss was quite different. He knew the right thing to say, at the right moment, and in the right way. He was a master communicator, and it was a beautiful thing to see him at work. He had great skill. When the word "wise" is used in the Bible of workers, it is used to describe "one who has masterful

---

[3] Bruce Waltke, *The Book of Proverbs*, vol. 1 (Grand Rapids: Eerdmans Publishing Co, 2004), 77.

[4] There is a close relationship of words in the wisdom complex with different words highlighting different facets. This is why different English translate passages differently and why at times they are virtually interchangeable.

understanding or skill"[5] (Ex 28:3, 31:6, 1 Kings 4:34). If we are going to be successful in the world and make a difference for the kingdom of God, we will need a masterful understanding of our trade and life in general.

We must aim for a high degree of competency in our trade. Masterful skill reminds me of a master craftsman who makes swords. He takes a blunt piece of scrap metal and carefully crafts it into a fine piece of weaponry. He knows the sides that need to be hammered hard and the ones that need delicate filing. With great skill he carefully crafts a sword that is strong, balanced, fit to the hand, and razor sharp. We are all craftsmen of some type and need to see the importance of great and precise skill. Skill is as important as anything else one does. No one picks a heart surgeon because he is a nice guy or tries real hard. Those are great characteristics to have, but not if he isn't good at what he does. Poor skill will nullify many other good qualities. If a person is going to be a heart surgeon he better be good at it, and it is the same for any other profession. Great skill is unfortunately an often overlooked goal that we need to see the importance of acquiring.

Great skill also implies a broad practical aptitude in life. Wisdom is not just having knowledge like many typically think, but also means being able to practically handle situations that come up. A person could memorize an economics book and still not have the practical skill to build a successful business. For example the Wright brothers had knowledge of the laws of aerodynamics, but they also had the wisdom to master the life situation they were in and bring about the crafting of an actual plane.[6] They knew how wings and drift worked, but more than that they were able to put plans into action and motivate others to accomplish tasks. They had a pragmatic aptitude that when coupled with their skillful ingenuity created significant results.

Practical skill in life plays out significantly in knowing how to work with other people. The wise person knows when to be patient (Prov 19:11), when to correct (Prov 9:8), when to hold the tongue (Prov 10:19), and when to give a gift (Prov 18:16).

---

[5] Ernst Jenni, and Claus Westermann. *Theological Lexicon of the Old Testament* (Peabody, MA: Hendrickson Publishers, 1997), 420.

[6] Waltke, *The Book of Proverbs*, vol. 1, 77.

Masterful skill in our work goes hand in hand with working effectively with those around us to achieve a desired end. We do not work in isolation and are almost always dependent on working with others to get things done. Great practical skill in our trade and surrounding is a necessity to succeed in our work.

8.3 Shrewdness

When Jesus prepared his disciples for their missionary journey he said to them, "I am sending you out like sheep among wolves. Therefore be as shrewd as snakes and as innocent as doves" (Matthew 10:16). Such advice may seem odd at first, but Jesus tells his disciples to be shrewd as snakes, because he knows they are going to be opposed, attacked, manipulated, lied to, and falsely accused. They are going to endure similar treatment as Jesus, and they need to be on guard. To work skillfully in the world will also require us to be shrewd.

The word for shrewd in the passage above could easily be translated "wise," but "shrewd" fits the context better as the metaphor of snakes suggests the "craftiness" of a snake is in view (Gen 3:1).[7] This shrewdness reminds there is more required in work than being nice and naively thinking others are going to do what's right. We also need sharp thinking that can be cunning and prevent wolves from hurting and hindering.

For some to hear that they are to be shrewd at work or in any part of life, or that the Bible encourages it, may be a bit of a shock. We will need to clarify this concept, because God honoring shrewdness is a delicate issue, but first we will look at some examples of shrewdness in the Bible. One example is when King Solomon is approached by two women prostitutes having a dispute over the death and custody of their children, and they wanted a ruling from Solomon. The full account is in 1 King 3:16-28

Now two prostitutes came to the king and stood before him. One of them said, "My lord, this woman and I live in the

---

[7] R.T. France, *The Gospel of Matthew* (Grand Rapids: Eerdmans, 2007), 388.

same house. I had a baby while she was there with me. The third day after my child was born, this woman also had a baby. We were alone; there was no one in the house but the two of us. During the night this woman's son died because she lay on him. So she got up in the middle of the night and took my son from my side while I your servant was asleep. She put him by her breast and put her dead son by my breast. The next morning, I got up to nurse my son-- and he was dead! But when I looked at him closely in the morning light, I saw that it wasn't the son I had borne." The other woman said, "No! The living one is my son; the dead one is yours." But the first one insisted, "No! The dead one is yours; the living one is mine." And so they argued before the king. The king said, "This one says, 'My son is alive and your son is dead,' while that one says, 'No! Your son is dead and mine is alive.'" Then the king said, "Bring me a sword." So they brought a sword for the king. He then gave an order: "Cut the living child in two and give half to one and half to the other." The woman whose son was alive was filled with compassion for her son and said to the king, "Please, my lord, give her the living baby! Don't kill him!" But the other said, "Neither I nor you shall have him. Cut him in two!" Then the king gave his ruling: "Give the living baby to the first woman. Do not kill him; she is his mother." When all Israel heard the verdict the king had given, they held the king in awe, because they saw that he had wisdom from God to administer justice.

This was a wise and shrewd way to discern the truth and cut to the heart of a matter. There are times where wolves with mal-intent will try to harm or wrong another, and a wise and shrewd statement or action can protect others and prevent evil. Solomon gave a shrewd verdict that wasted no time getting to the heart of the matter and revealing the hidden intention of the wicked woman. He dealt shrewdly with a woman who was herself shrewd, and his decision suppressed evil and rendered justice to a woman, child, and community.

Shrewdness doesn't belong to Solomon alone. Jesus also demonstrated shrewdness. He would often challenge those challenging him and give just enough of a reply to cut to the heart of a matter and keep himself from being trapped. He would skillfully answer questions on paying taxes (Matt 22:19) and was cautious revealing his messiahship (Matt 16:20).

Another example of Jesus' shrewdness comes when his opponents question whose authority he was performing his miracles (Mark 11:27-33). Recognizing a trap, Jesus asked them a question saying, "John's baptism—was it from heaven or from men? Tell me." If they answered from heaven then the obvious questions would be why didn't they believe John (who testified about Jesus), but if they say from men then the crowd will turn against them because they viewed John as a prophet. Jesus's opponents refused to answer his question, so Jesus refused to answer their question. He deals with their question with wisdom and shrewdness. He is cautious in what he says to them and asks a question that puts responsibility on them to clarify their intentions. His actions help reveal their intent and prevent them from trapping him.

These examples show the wise acting shrewdly when confronted with antagonistic people, so that they are not manipulated or hindered. They acted boldly so as to get to the heart of the issue quickly, decisively, accurately, and effectively. It was their shrewd use of wisdom that allowed them to do this.

Before turning to contemplate specific ways we can apply shrewdness, one qualification needs to be added. We are to be "shrewd as snakes" but also as "innocent as doves." The wisdom and shrewdness that Jesus calls his disciples to is one that is without sin. It is without fault, without harm, and without evil. It is pure, holy, and right, and does not contradict any other characteristic (holiness, righteousness, purity, truthfulness, etc) that God calls us to. It is much different from the shrewdness the world demonstrates in destroying others while advantaging itself.

Godly shrewdness does not hurt, oppress, or take advantage of others. To do so would be wickedness. It is a shrewdness that is blameless and righteous. It is a shrewdness that is innocent as a dove. To be successful in the world one must be shrewd, but it requires special shrewdness to not be hindered by evil people while also not bringing disrepute upon oneself or associates. In the words of Leon Morris, we "must live in a way as to commend the message, not carelessly as non-Christian people generally do."[8] God-honoring shrewdness requires a delicate balance between shrewdness and innocence.

These two truths of being shrewd yet innocent bind two important aspects of work together which R.T. France effectively summarizes saying, "Christians are not to be gullible simpletons. But neither are they to be rogues. It demands not naivety but an irreproachable honesty."[9] Maintaining these two aspects is no doubt very difficult and led J.C. Ryle to say, "There are few of our Lord's commands which it is so difficult to use correctly as this one. There is a line marked out for us, but it is a line that requires great skill to define."[10]

While it is difficult to define all the nuances, there are a few ways we would do well to use shrewdness in our work. The first is by asking direct questions on the issue at hand. This is exactly what my boss did, and he was able to cut to the chase and find out exactly where my customer was at. It is also what we see with Solomon and Jesus. If we think we are being manipulated asking direct questions is the first place to go. People who fail to ask direct questions fail to clarify the situation and leave themselves vulnerable to being easily misled.

A second way is to require the person to do something that shows their sincerity. Solomon asked something to be done to the child that he knew the true mother could not allow. Jesus was not willing to answer a question until the elders first answered his. In the same way, when we are concerned or question the people we are working with, it could be wisdom to require something of them that will help us better gage what their true intentions are. When my boss suspected my prospective client may be using me he actually asked them to sign a document that would allow us to contact their current vendor for clarifying information about their services. When they refused to do this he had good reason to suspect things were not going anywhere. This revelation helped

---

[8] Leon Morris, *The Gospel According to Matthew* (Grand Rapids: Eerdmans Publishing Company, 1992), 253.

[9] R.T. France, *Matthew,* Tyndale New Testament Commentaries (Grand Rapids: Eerdmans Publishing Company, 1985), 182.

[10] J.C. Ryle, *Matthew* (Wheaton: Crossway, 1993), 74.

him see that a deeper and even more direct question needed to be asked.

People are not always upfront, can have hidden agendas, and often do not easily back down from bad intentions. There will be times in work where it will be appropriate and even necessary to be shrewd, yet it must be exercised with great care as it can easily lead one into disrepute. Asking clear direct questions that do not beat around the bush or requiring a person to do something that clarifies where they are at are a couple ways we can exercise shrewdness that is innocent as a dove.

8.4 Knowledge

I once heard it said that people are often as innocent as snakes and shrewd as doves. In some ways this statement would describe one of the worst moments of my sales career. It came while training with another rep named Leslie, whose greatest asset was her domineering personality. As we went to meet with her client, her last words before entering his office were, "Today I will overpower him, and he will sign my contract."

The meeting started awkwardly and quickly got uncomfortable. I soon realized the customer didn't want to meet with her and had reluctantly done so because of her stubbornness. He was, shall we say, less than enthusiastic to see us. On top of this, after just a few minutes, even I (the new guy) realized that the customer was pretty savvy with his services and had some needs that Leslie wasn't helping with (but she didn't realize it, because she was trying to "overpower him"). It was obvious that Leslie did not understand her product enough to know how it could help him!

When she began to sense a deepening frustration from the customer, she decided to press him and threw out an unbelievable ultimatum. She looked sternly at him and said, "You are wasting my time, and if you do not sign this contract right now I am going to take all my expertise and leave you to fend for yourself." (At this point I thought about leaving but realized there was no way we would be in there much longer!) The customer quickly made it very clear our services were not what he needed, he did not trust us, and he never wanted to see us again. Ironically, Leslie used almost the exact words of my manager, yet experienced a staggeringly different effect. Shrewdness without knowledge is useless.

Knowledge is the power and ability to accurately grasp and retain information. True knowledge also means that one is able to understand the relevance of the knowledge. For example knowledge of the Bible means one knows where certain passages are located and what they mean, but they can also use them in appropriate situations. We must have knowledge of the field we are in because knowledge is the foundation our service is built on.

In talking about practical skill earlier some could assume that practical skill makes knowledge unimportant. This is not true, and wisdom requires a person to both grasp concepts and have practical know how. Memorizing the bible may not make you a saint, but can you be a saint without knowing the Bible? Can you have great skill at anything without thoroughly knowing the core concepts of that field? In the case above, Leslie made an embarrassing practical move, because she did not understand her product and how it could help her customer.

Wisdom to get things done always involves the ability to think correctly about subjects. The Wright brothers had an ability to practically get things done in the world, but without the knowledge of the laws of aerodynamics they would have been unsuccessful. The knowledge of aerodynamics helps the engineer make sound planes. Knowledge of geometry and math helps the architect make stable buildings. Knowledge of engines helps the mechanic fix the car. Knowledge of history helps a president make informed decisions on policies. Knowledge of theology and biblical languages helps the pastor lead his people effectively. In general the more knowledge we have, the better and more informed our decisions will be on a variety of subjects.

Knowledge will also provide guidance that determines where to concentrate effort (Prov 19:2), and this direction can increase effectiveness (Prov 24:5). Many people zealously spin their wheels in work because they lack the knowledge to know where they should focus. If Leslie had rightly understood her product she could have focused her efforts on overpowering her customer with a great solution. Knowledge is power, and as a lumberjack's effectiveness grows when he sharpens his axe, so also our effectiveness is sharpened by growing in knowledge (Ecc 10:10).

8.5 Prudence

Prudence means that one is careful in their actions. It is being cautious and giving much thought to what is done or said. A prudent person doesn't act rashly or impulsively but rather in accordance with what he discerns is best. Foolish people believe anything, but the prudent give thought to their ways (Prov 14:15). Prudence undertakes responsibility with great care and conscientiousness.

Prudent people manage wisely because they have the foresight to look ahead. They are not living for the moment, and they consider the future as well as the present effect of their actions. The prudent person "notices everything in advance, and governs his actions accordingly."[11] They look ahead to problems or dangers and prepare for them (Proverbs 22:3), so they are not caught off guard and overtaken by them.

The prudent are often contrasted with the simple (Prov 1:4, 17:2, 19:25). The simple are those who believe anything and are easily misled. The simple do not give careful thought to their ways and are blown and tossed every which way (Prov 1:32). They do whatever is easiest. It is the simple who fail to properly consider problems, and they suffer for it (Prov 22:3).

An example of prudent decision making comes from Mike, who started an internet based company in the dot com boom of the late 1990's. Early on people were flocking to his company for his service and making money was easy, but he knew things could not go this way forever. If he was going to have a lasting business he would need to use this unique time of prosperity to prepare for the future. While his competitors were sinking money into sports cars for advertisement, decorating offices like Fortune 500 companies, and living a plush lifestyle, Mike was being very conservative paying off debt, making sure the company had a solid infrastructure, and saving for future needs. Many laughed at his

---

[11] Brakel, 129.

caution, but when the dot com bust happened Mike was in a unique position not only to remain profitable but to also purchase his competitors at bargain rates. His prudent foresight led him to plan for adversity and position himself for long term success rather than living for the moment.

Like Mike, we need to not just live for the moment but give prudent thought to what lays down the road and how to get where we want to be. Many will fail in their work, because their decisions are based on momentary fancies, but the prudent consider how today's actions prepare for tomorrow's goal.

8.6 Diligence

If prudence is thinking ahead to the best plan of action, diligence is carrying out that plan. Diligence is the constant and attentive effort to accomplish a goal. The diligent person is able to focus on set goals and do what needs to be done to accomplish those goals. They measure each step in the process and then faithfully implement the strategy.[12]

Oswald Chambers said, "Before we conquer the world we must first conquer the self."[13] Diligence is one part of wisdom focused more on overcoming the self than external things. The diligent are able to conquer the self and do what needs to be done when it needs to be done. They are self starters that work without needing someone to goad or threaten them (Prov 6:6-8). Not only does the diligent person start well but he also stays on top of his work and doesn't let it get out of control (Prov 24:30-31). They are faithful to work, because they have the self-discipline to push aside distractions.

In Proverbs the diligent are contrasted with the sluggards who can always find a reason not to work or wait a little longer before starting (Prov 6:9-11). The sluggard fails to finish the simplest task (Prov 19:24) and always finds an excuse, even if it is

---

[12] Daniel J. Estes, *Handbook on the Wisdom Books and Psalms* (Grand Rapids: Baker Academic, 2005), 236.

[13] Oswald Sanders, *Spiritual Leadership* (Chicago: Moody Publishers, 1994), 52.

outlandish (Prov 22:13). Their way is always blocked with difficulty (Prov 15:19), and each day they fail to accomplish their work; it mounts and gets more difficult. Sluggards come in all shapes and sizes. Some are obvious, but perhaps the most prevalent sluggards are disguised as busy bodies. They are always doing something, answering a phone or email, or looking online, yet failing to do the things that are most necessary at the time.

Diligence is not flashy, but an ordinary principle essential to success. Daniel Estes said, "Diligence motivates a person to move quickly and accept challenges, to stay focused on what is crucial in the long run rather than living for what is convenient at the present, and to grasp decisively the opportunities that God presents."[14] Rightly seeing today's work as an opportunity from God is key to grasping opportunities decisively and diligently staying focused with constant and attentive effort on what is most important. Distracting temptations are always present, but the diligent stay focused.

Such self-denying diligence should be viewed with faith and excitement, because in the end, it is the diligent that reap abundantly (Prov 10:4, 12:24). Thomas Watson said, "God blesses a man's diligence, not his laziness."[15] We have an obligation to work hard, and as we do there should be an eager anticipation that God will use our drive and faithfulness to bring about the results we hope for and desire. A farmer must be diligent to plant seeds today to have a crop tomorrow. Likewise, today's work is the seed that bring tomorrow's harvest. It is the diligent farmer with seed in the ground that joyfully anticipates a future crop. As we are diligent, we can joyfully anticipate fruit from our work.

8.7 Discernment

Discernment is the ability to evaluate and comprehend something and then make a judgment about it. It is looking at different things and choosing between good and bad, right and wrong, or even good and better. Every day we are confronted with

---

[14] Estes, 236.
[15] Leland Ryken, *Worldly Saints* (Grand Rapids: Zondervan, 1990), 34.

the necessity of making decisions, and the quality of those decisions directly affects the outcome of our work. Discerning the right way to walk is an extremely important gifting to cultivate.

A main component of good discernment is the ability to look past what clouds a situation and see what is at the core. The discerning are not fooled by mere appearance nor are they distracted by matters of secondary importance (Prov 28:11). They see past these, and their focused insight on essential matters allows them to make good decisions for productive and enduring work (Prov 24:3).

Joseph is a great example of a discerning man. After interpreting Pharaoh's dream of the future famine, he tells Pharaoh to save a fifth of the land's produce for the next seven years to prepare for the famine. That is the equivalent of saving twenty percent of one's income for seven years! No doubt a great sacrifice, but it was with such discernment Joseph clearly understood the severity of the problem and made the best judgment on how the nation could survive. With such discernment, Joseph effectively governed a nation and delivered many people from devastation (Gen 41:33-34).

Discernment is just as useful today. John was a commercial real estate developer in the early stages of developing the first piece of property in a promising new area. The land was bought, plans were drawn, and the construction was full speed ahead when the city informed them they were violating numerous city codes.

The codes were old and outdated and seemed like nonsense to the developers. As John and his partners began to talk, they realized the codes did not forbid their work but would only result in financial penalties. They decided what they had to gain was far greater than what the penalties would cost, but John also discerned there could be a huge problem if their decision to break these codes went against the opinion of the community. This could result in even greater damage.

John decided to pole the community and get extensive advice on what they thought of the issue and how the project should be done. The end result found that the entire community was in favor of the project, and after seeing the developers' care and interest for their community, they embraced it even more. His decision allowed the team to continue the work and win the approval of the community.

It was John's discernment that helped him see opportunity in what initially seemed like a dead end, but just as critical as seeing the opportunity was recognizing and not minimizing the potential and legitimate danger of losing the support of the community. This allowed him to walk through the situation in a way that did not leave him, his company, or his project in disrepute. His discernment allowed him to look squarely at the facts of the difficult situation and determine a successful way to navigate the delicate situation.

Discernment requires a person to focus on the actual situation and not a wrong view or hoped for view of the situation. Many fail to exercise good discernment, because they fail to assess situations accurately. Daniel Estes said, the discerning "do not overestimate their own capabilities nor do they underrate the difficulties and dangers involved in a given course of action."[16] Good discernment requires a sober perspective that acknowledges real difficulties and potential shortcomings. Foolish people believe anything but the discerning base judgments on accurate assessments (Prov 15:14). Only through honest evaluations of the real life scenario is good discernment exercised.

8.8 Humility

Humility is having an appropriately modest estimation of our thoughts, ideas, deeds, and abilities. It is perhaps best explained as the opposite of pride. Pride is thinking too highly of oneself, and it has no regard for others. Biblically speaking the perils of pride cannot be more serious: "God opposes the proud but gives grace to the humble" (James 4:6, 1 Peter 5:5).

To be successful in work there must be a degree of humility. Pride often comes before ruin (Prov 16:18), and the destructive nature of pride expresses itself in many ways. Proud people refuse to listen to others, care only for themselves, and

---

[16] Daniel Estes, *Handbook on the Wisdom Books and Psalms* (Grand Rapids: Baker Academic, 2005), 233.

think their way is the only way. Pride causes quarrels and strife (Prov 13:10) and can lead to walking down paths others are not willing to follow. This is largely what happened to Leslie as she tried to work with her customer. In her pride she tried dominating the customer and was not hearing his needs. She had one agenda, he had another, and the consequences were costly.

Business and work revolve around helping others, and if we are too proud to truly listen to them we are going to struggle in our work. Pride keeps us from both understanding and receiving from others. This in turn will cause people to dislike working with us and to even push away from us.

Peter managed a small office of about thirteen guys. In his proud estimation he was a great leader and thought his guys enjoyed taking his directions, but Peter's boss began noticing a significant decline in the team's performance and started asking questions. It turned out Peter had been ignoring some of the needs of his guys because he thought these needs were unimportant, and he refused to listen to their ideas for change. As a result, the team had grown frustrated with their work and their performance declined.

It grieved Peter to discover the problems were due to his uncaring leadership. By humbling himself, sharing his mistakes, and resolving to work with his team, the team embraced him, grew together, and they soon began pacing with other strong teams. Pride had destroyed the team, but humility brought restoration.

Real humility not only considers others but actively seeks advice from them. This is a repeated theme in Proverbs. The fool trusts in his own mind (Prov 28:26), but the wise person listens and learns from those around them (Prov 1:5, 8:33, 13:1, 22:17). Life is difficult, and we will need the help of others. Whether we are perplexed at a particular situation or want to be informed on a topic, seeking the counsel and guidance of others can ensure a successful path (Prov 11:14). It is not weakness to ask others for advice; it is humility, and such humility will give much insight on successfully navigating the various situations we encounter. This is the main reason "humility comes before honor" (Prov 18:12).

8.9 How to Gain Wisdom

A few years ago a friend's sister got married, and the new in-law made a string of really bad and really noticeably bad decisions. For his poor judgment the family cruelly nicknamed him "stuck on stupid." Assessing their character for calling him that is not our goal here, but assessing the validity of the statement is. We can get buried in difficult situations, often because of our own stupidity, and despond if we will ever get out of it or even more if we will ever grow wiser. One pastor I know would often say in jest, "I can repent of sin, but stupid is forever." That's a great line to rib people with, but not a line to summarize biblical teaching. Biblically speaking no one is "stuck on stupid." Thankfully wisdom can be gained, and we should pursue it more than we pursue money or riches (Prov 16:16).

There are numerous ways that wisdom can be gained. It comes by pondering life and evaluating the positive and negative things experienced, as the author of Proverbs repeatedly shows (Prov 24:30-32). It comes with time; People learn as they live (Pro 20:29). It comes from enduring difficulties and discipline, and some of our hardest times are the moments we learn the greatest lessons. It comes by listening to parents and elders (Prov 1:8), studying the works of the wise (Prov 22:17), heeding advice (Prov 19:20), walking with wise friends (Prov 13:20), prayer (James 1:5), and a host of other things.

Wisdom also comes from the cumulative effect of all the things discussed. As we grow in knowledge, it affects our ability to discern situations and prudently gauge the future. As we grow in prudence, it affects our diligence, discernment, and humility. As we grow in working diligently, it leads to greater knowledge and discernment. Growing in one area strengthens the other areas. When desiring to grow in wisdom the best plan may be to pick one area and devote ourselves to it.

All these aspects of wisdom affect our ability to successfully navigate the world, but there is one last aspect of wisdom that is possibly the most important. The foundation of learning wisdom is learning to fear the Lord. The fear of the Lord is the key to all aspects of wisdom. Proverbs 1:7 says, "The fear of the Lord is the beginning of knowledge," and Derek Kidner said that "the 'fear of the Lord'—is not a mere beginner's step in wisdom, to be left behind, but the prerequisite of every right attitude."[17] The fear of the Lord is the key to rightly seeing how God has ordered the world and intended it to function.[18] If we want to live wisely it begins with turning to the Lord. The fear of the Lord affects all aspects of wisdom. It instills discernment because we know there are good and evil decisions, prudence because one day we will give an account to the Lord for everything done, diligence because any day could be the day for that account, humility because we are dependent on God, and shrewdness because we know our service to God will be resisted.

The fear of the Lord also leads to seeing our need for a savior and the wisdom found in Christ. Christ has become for us wisdom (1 Cor 1:30), and in him are all the treasures of wisdom and knowledge (Col 2:3). John Owen said, "It is by the knowing of (Christ) we become acquainted with the wisdom of God."[19] If we want wisdom it begins with turning to Christ and walking with him. Deciding to walk with Christ is in fact the wisest and most important decision we can make; it enriches our life in every way (1 Cor 1:5), including the way we work.

8.10 Conclusion

There are many challenges that confront us in the world and make our work difficult. Things are never easy, and challenges will come from the world and ourselves. If we are going to succeed in working for the glory of God we will have to get things done, and this requires wisdom. Wisdom is an appointed means of grace to help navigate the world successfully, and it involves characteristics like skill, shrewdness, knowledge, prudence, diligence, and humility. These characteristics help guide us to successfully accomplish our work in a manner that pleases God.

---

[17] Derek Kidner, *The Wisdom of Proverbs, Job, and Ecclesiastes* (Downers Grove: Inter-Varsity press, 1985), 19.

[18] Ibid. This is a paraphrase of Kidner.

[19] John Owen, *The Works of John Owen,* Vol 2 (Carlisle, PA: Banner of Truth Trust, 1997), 80.

Wisdom navigates the vast array of precarious situations we find ourselves in. Though we may lack wisdom at times, God in his grace gives the ability to grow in it, and we should make use of the means he has provided. True wisdom centers on Christ and ultimately comes from walking with him in the fear of the Lord. As we walk in wisdom with Christ, we will experience better discernment, greater prudence, stronger discipline, deeper knowledge, and much more. Faith in Christ leads to true wisdom, and balances the twin poles of working effectively and honoring God.

Chapter 8 Discussion Questions

1. What aspect of wisdom are you weakest in? Which are you strongest in?

2. What aspect of wisdom was most surprising to hear about?

3. Is there an issue in your work that you need help determining what is the best way to handle? What are some biblical ways you can get help with it?

Chapter 9

Break Time—Finding Rest for the Weary Soul

"Remember the Sabbath day by keeping it holy. Six days you shall labor and do all your work, but the seventh day is a Sabbath to the LORD your God. On it you shall not do any work, neither you, nor your son or daughter, nor your manservant or maidservant, nor your animals, nor the alien within your gates. For in six days the LORD made the heavens and the earth, the sea, and all that is in them, but he rested on the seventh day. Therefore the LORD blessed the Sabbath day and made it holy."
Exodus 20:8-11

Sean came to college on the highest scholarship the university awarded and began an ambitious plan to graduate in microbiology in two years. His goal was to enroll in med-school as soon as he could so he could start making big money as soon as possible. He had everything planned out, and achieving his ambitious goals required taking twenty two hours of pre-med classes his first semester, while also working a part time job. He was diligent with his game plan and sacrificed many luxuries like weekends off, time with friends, and on many nights sleep. There were a few bumps along the way but for the most part things went as planned, at least for the first eight weeks. Then reality came crashing down.

Already weary from a grueling schedule, he pulled a string of all-nighters to study for his midterms. His lack of sleep led to an inability to focus and think clearly. During his exams he could hardly read his tests much less think of the right answers. After returning from his disastrous midterms, he fell asleep and slept straight through the next three days of classes. He was taken to the doctor by concerned roommates and given strict orders by the doctors to rest. He had exhausted himself in every way.

Sean's case is an extreme situation, and while most of us don't take things quite that far, we are prone to a dull burnout that hangs over and clouds our life like a dense morning fog. We make ambitious goals and run ourselves down to meet those goals. We feel exhausted but just can't afford to take time off. We have talked much about the importance of work, the value God places upon it, and the great opportunity it presents to do much good, and this should inspire us to be passionate about work, but any teaching on work would be incomplete if it did not talk about the need to rest.

People fail to rest for a variety of reasons. Some allow their trust in themselves and their work to keep them from taking time off. Others think that by resting they are doing something wrong. They boast of their work ethic as if work without rest is noble. People fail to see the importance of rest and think that doing so is wrong or weak. Tim Hansel articulates these problems with his book titled, *When I Relax I Feel Guilty.*[1] It shows how confused people are about the place of rest in their lives. They can talk about work and working hard, but resting perplexes them.

Such thinking reflects an unbiblical view of work, and one that does not honor God. Rest is important to mankind because as B.B. Warfield said, "Man needs it. It blesses his life."[2] Work is difficult and painful, and in order to be productive one must rest. While some people think rest is a luxury they cannot afford, the truth is they can scarcely afford not to rest.[3] Given the tendency to misunderstand rest we need to make sure we have a right understanding of it. If we are going to glorify God by doing work that matters we will also have to learn how to rest to the glory of God.

---

[1] Tim Hansel, *When I Relax I Feel Guilty* (Elgen, IL: David C Cook), 1979.

[2] B.B. Warrfield, "The Foundations of the Sabbath in the Word of God" in B.B. Warfield, *Selected Shorter Writings*, vol 1 (Phillipsburg: P&R Publishing, 1970), 309.

[3] Bruce Waltke, *An Old Testament Theology*, (Grand Rapids: Zondervan, 2007), 421.

9.1 Biblical Ways of Resting

I am person who tends to get engrossed in work and overlook resting. I have worked too long many nights and have even completely missed major holidays. The worst was forgetting to plan for Easter and having to rush to the store on the way home from church to buy some burgers to throw on the grill. It is sad, and I am ashamed of it, but it is true. Over the years I have grown a great deal in this area of my life, and one thing that helped me is seeing rest is so important it is commanded in the Bible. There are even different kinds of rest prescribed, and we do well to understand these. The different kinds are daily rest, weekly rest, and what I call special rest.

The first pattern of rest is a daily rest and is seen in Genesis 1. On each day of creation God does a creative work, and then the Bible says, "And there was evening, and there was morning" (Gen 1:5, 8, 13, 19, 23, 31). This phrase indicates a concluding time of rest or leisure on each day. Speaking of this rest Leland Ryken says, "In the actual account of creation, God rests from his creative work after each day, setting up a rhythm of work and rest or leisure."[4] This rhythm of daily rests should be present each day to provide for various needs. It sets a pattern for the sleep we need each day. In addition to sleep, this rest also provides a context for leisure activities that enrich our life like times with family, friends, and hobbies. This rest provides a basis to take care of spiritual needs on a daily basis. Jesus modeled this, as he would often go to solitary places to pray (Mark 1:35). The demands and responsibilities of each day are great and make it imperative to find consistent daily rest for our physical and spiritual needs. Like Jesus, we need to know when it is appropriate to get away and rest (Mark 6:31).

Another type of rest in scripture is what I call "special rest." These times are seasonal, prolonged, and do not have exact parallels today. The Old Testament mentions special feasts that were held in different seasons of the year (Ex 23:14-16) in which work was limited (Num 28:18, 25, 26, 29:1, 12) and even prohibited for prolonged times (Exod 23:15, Lev 23:6-7, 34-35).

---

[4] Leland Ryken, *Redeeming the Time,* 160.

They were times of joy (Deut 16:11, 14) and celebrations (Lev 23:39, Deut 16:15) that centered on worshiping God and enjoying the fruit of one's labors with others. These feasts show a prescription for regular and consistent periods of prolonged rest at various seasons of the year. They are probably similar to our vacations, or Christmas, and would probably most resemble our Thanksgiving holiday when it is properly observed.[5] They were important and meaningful times whose pattern we should not neglect or consider unimportant.[6]

The other type of rest mentioned in the Bible is weekly rest, which is the Sabbath. The Sabbath finds its beginning in Genesis 2 where God works for six days, and on the seventh day he rests. Genesis 2:2-3 says, "By the seventh day God had finished the work he had been doing; so on the seventh day he rested from all his work. And God blessed the seventh day and made it holy, because on it he rested from all the work of creating that he had done." With this rest God sets a weekly cycle of working six days and resting on the seventh (Ex 16:26). Taking an entire day off each week is a normal and God honoring rest that we should observe.

These are three different ways to rest, and from these we see some of the benefits of resting. Of all the types of rest mentioned in the Bible, Sabbath rest is the one most extensively described, and therefore the one that provides the fullest and most accurate theology of rest. For this reason we will look at Sabbath rest in detail to better understand the many important parts of rest, and the first thing we will look at is how stringently to observe rest.

---

[5] Ibid, 206. Ryken suggests a connection that I take and am more specific in my application of it than he is.

[6] While these feasts set a pattern of rest, we should not try to emulate the exact practices prescribed by them such as the events, the diet, or the customs. These feasts are part of the ceremonial law that was fulfilled in Christ. Like animal sacrifices, these feasts point to Christ and find fulfillment in him and do not need to be observed as precisely spelled out in the Old Testament. So while we do not need to observe the practice exactly, we are wise to incorporate the principal of rest, worship, and feasting into our lives.

9.2 Is It Right to Work on Sundays?

As we shift to talk about Sabbath rest, my ultimate goal is to talk about how the Sabbath is a blessing and how such rest can benefit one's life, but inevitably the question arises of "How strictly should Sabbath rest be observed?" For instance, some restaurants are open on Sundays, some are not, and this leads us to ask, "Should I, or should I not work on Sundays?" For this reason we will deal with the question up front.

First off, Sabbath rest should continue to be observed because it is a creation ordinance. It was instituted in creation (Gen 2:2, 3), follows God's example (Gen 2:2), is listed in the Ten Commandments (Exod 20:1-17), and affirmed a place in Christ's Lordship as he is Lord over the Sabbath (Mark 2:27, 28).[7] This means that we should continue to observe this pattern of rest.

So then, how can Christians even presume to work on Sundays in light of the ongoing nature of the Sabbath? This is a complex question, and an overly simplified answer is: The Sabbath pattern should be observed, but Jesus frees us from legalistic and overly stringent observation of it.

In Jesus' time no law had been more formalized and encrusted with meaning than the Sabbath. On the Sabbath a person couldn't walk more than 1200 yards (Acts 1:12), aid an animal that had fallen in a pit (Luke 14:5), or even light a fire (Exod 35:3). Such things were considered work, which was forbidden. Sabbath observance had turned into a list of do's and don'ts that became a hindrance rather than a blessing.

In the midst of such tradition and legalism Jesus provided a stark correction. The Pharisees questioned him about the Sabbath when they saw his disciples passing through a field and picking grain to eat with their hands, which was forbidden on the Sabbath. Replying to their questions Jesus said, "The Sabbath was made for man, not man for the Sabbath" (Mark 2:27). This response does

---

[7] John Murray, "The Sabbath Institution," in John Murray, *The Collected Writings of John Murray*, vol 1 (Carlisle: Banner of Truth Trust, 1976), 206-208.

not indicate the Sabbath is to be forsaken, but rather it puts the Sabbath in place as a tool for people.

Jesus shows the intent of the Sabbath was not for producing righteousness or binding people, but as a means of benefiting them. People are not to be bound by the Sabbath, because they were not made to be conformed to the Sabbath. The Sabbath was made for their good. Just as Jesus showed the true intent of the law by forbidding not just adultery but even looking lustfully at a woman, and showing murder is not just killing but also hating, so now he transforms our understanding of the Sabbath. While he increased the standards of adultery and murder, he brings a laxity to the Sabbath that shows it is about bringing life not hindering it.

We are to observe Sabbath rest, because it is good for us, not because we are bound by it. Since we are not bound by the Sabbath, it is permissible for us to work on it. This is why Westminster Larger Catechism 117 encourages observance of the Sabbath, but also permits the performance of "works of necessity." It is permissible to do necessary work like a soldier standing guard, a pastor ministering to people, a medical doctor standing on call, and yes, those inevitable emergencies that arise at the office.

If analyzed more closely it is also possible to see "works of necessity" encompass many other things. Jesus disciples picked and ate grain on the Sabbath, but this couldn't be considered a necessity as they could go without food for one day. So works of necessity are not just those works that are absolutely necessary for survival but can also include things that enhance life. John Frame says works of necessity are not "a necessity for human survival, but a necessity for maintaining the general quality of human life as it exists in our time and culture."[8]

Events that require working on the Sabbath will arise, and when they do they should be the exception rather than the norm, but they should also be done with faith that they are permitted. Employees should seek rest for themselves, but when a work of necessity arises they should not disdain their employer for it. They should instead work diligently with faith. In turn employers should

---

[8] John Frame, *Doctrine of the Christian Life* (Phillipsburg: P&R Publishing, 2008), 549.

recognize the appropriateness of providing rest and making sure their workers have another time for it.

The Sabbath should be observed as a day of rest, but it is not to be observed with the same strictness of the Old Testament. It can be difficult to have a balanced view of this rest, and for that reason people must avoid the common errors of either legalistic observation or unholy abdication. Rightly observing rest but not being bound by it requires great wisdom. Richard Baxter gives helpful advice on how to evaluate if a person is rightly observing the Sabbath or not. He says,

> I will first look at a man's positive duties on the Lord's Day how he hears and reads and prays and spends his time, how he instructs and helps his family, and if he is diligent in seeking God and ply his heavenly business, I shall be very backward to judge him for a word or action about worldly things that fall on the by.[9]

Baxter essentially says that if a person values the Sabbath and diligently makes provision to observe it, but at times is called into duty, we should be very slow to judge him for it. On the other hand if a man treats the Sabbath with little regard and sees no difference on it than any other day, then we should point out his need to experience God-honoring rest.

The balance of grace and devotion to the Sabbath should color the way we see all rest, be it a Sabbath, vacation, holiday, or morning devotion. Rest is prescribed for our good and can be detrimental if we do not observe it. If we do not observe a time of rest we should have a very good reason for breaking the pattern, and yet we do recognize there is grace for extenuating circumstances.

---

[9] J.I. Packer, "The Puritans and the Lord's Day," in J.I. Packer, editor, *Puritan Paperbacks,* vol 1 (Phillipsburg: P&R Publishing, 2000), 99.

9.3 Goals and Benefits of Rest

Matthew Henry said "The Sabbath is a sacred and divine institution, and we must receive and embrace it as a privilege and benefit, not as a task and a drudger."[10] The Sabbath can easily be viewed as a hollow command that only burdens and complicates our work. If we are going to fight against such thinking and rightly value and observe the Sabbath, we must be captured by its benefits. These benefits show the privilege and importance of rest, but moreover they show what real God-honoring rest should consist of. The main benefits are rest, reflection, and edification.

9.3.1 Rest

The essential meaning of the word Sabbath means to rest and to cease from work. For that reason it is logical that this be the first important benefit. With great imagery B.B. Warfield explains,

> This is the day on which the tired body rests from its appointed labor; on which the worn spirit finds opportunity for recuperation; an oasis in the desert of earthly cares, when we can escape for a moment from the treadmill toil of daily life and, at leisure from ourselves, refresh our souls in God.[11]

Rest should be an oasis to us, a breath of fresh air that reenergizes us, and we should be unashamed of it. We need to recognize our limitation and the ease with which we can drive ourselves into the dirt. When people are tired and push themselves too far they suffer for it and end up doing poor work. It is at these times the very thing that can make us most effective is to not work at all.

I am very aware of my tendency of pushing too hard on projects or deadlines and watching my work suffer. In these times it feels like there is so much to do I cannot take any time off. After staring at a spreadsheet on the computer screen for hours trying to

---

[10] Packer, 94.
[11] Warrfield, 308.

find where certain discrepancies may lie, I soon find myself in a concerned stare where I am too afraid to leave but too fatigued to do anything effectively. By foolishly pressing on in such a condition I neither get good work done nor find effective rest. When I take time to rest and refresh myself my work is more effective and also more enjoyable.

It can be very difficult to pull back from work, but we must humbly realize that we were not made to work without rest. It is imperative to rest, and for that reason we must protect such times. William McNamara said, "Possibly the greatest malaise in our country today is our neurotic compulsions to work."[12] This compulsion is also fed by today's technology. Cell phones buzz during dinner, text ding early in the morning, and emails find us even at the beach. We need real rest and not just time away from the office. Our rest is always being attacked, and we must be on guard so unwanted intruders don't break in.

Given our need for rest and our tendency to feel compelled to always work, I have found it just as important planning when *not* to work as it is planning when *to* work. Planning my days off, my lunch breaks, and even 10 minute breaks throughout the day help ensure I am resting before hitting a breaking point (and planning these ensures I don't rest too much). I work toward these breaks, so when it is time for a break I need it. When it is time to come home and be with family I am ready for a break and can enjoy being with them. Planning these strategic brakes provides rest and allows me to enjoy other important parts of life.

Rest is a gift from God that we should enjoy, and it is a gift that we should allow others to enjoy too. Part of obeying the command to rest also involves giving rest to others (Deut 5:14). We should make sure those under our dominion such as employees, children, or even spouses are able to rest. God in his goodness gives us the gift of rest, and giving rest to others is a way we imitate God. This is why some say the keeping of the Sabbath is more directly aimed at governors of families and other superiors; they need to keep it not only for themselves, but also for those under them (WLC118).

---

[12] Hansel, 34.

God did not create people to work without ceasing. People need rest, and in his kindness God gave time for refreshing. The "joyful character of the day of rest brings home to the worshipper that his God is a kindly Master, who does not lay on men a yoke too heavy to bear."[13] We are grateful God is a kind master to us, and we should be kind masters to others affected by our care. If God grants rest to refresh us from our work, we should grant it to others without thinking them to be weak, uncommitted, or lazy employees. We need refreshing, and so do others.

9.3.2 Reflection

When God created the world he took time off, and it was in this time he reflected on what he did. This reflection is seen in the statement, "And God saw that it was good." God made light and saw it was good (Gen 1:4). He made the sea and saw it was good (1:10); he made plants, trees, and vegetation, and saw it was good (1:12). He also did this with day and night (1:18), animals of the sea, land, and sky, (1:21), and beast, livestock, and creeping things (1:25). This pattern shows that God took time to reflect on what he had done and delight in it. When resting we too should take intentional time to reflect on what is good in our work.

Reflecting on goodness in work is a key discipline that can transform our perception of work. Doing this has allowed me to be more aware of where God is at work and what has been done rather than what has not been done. It is an intentional time to fix our thoughts on good things (Phil 4:8). It is human nature to dwell on unfixed problems, which can quickly lead to discouragement. Reflecting on accomplishments brings encouragement and excitement.

Reflecting on work is good for a weary soul. It brings attention to the good things that have happened. It reminds of goals that have been met, the obstacles that have been hurdled, the progress made, and the lessons learned. It also allows us to consider how our work has blessed other people. Since blessing

---

[13] Walter Eichrodt, *Theology of the Old Testament*, vol 1 (Philadelphia: The Westminster Press, 1961), 133.

others is central to our work, it is good for us to think about it, and this consideration seems the closest parallel to what God did in creation.

Our reflection shouldn't just end with considering our work alone but should also consider God's work, and how he has been faithful to us. We should consider the prayers that have been answered and the way he has helped us through the challenging thorns and thistle. In the midst of all we labor for, it is ultimately God that causes it to bear fruit, and taking time to reflect on God's faithful provision will give faith for future work.

9.3.3 Edification: Being Built Up

I love to watch football on Sundays. It is one of my favorite ways to rest. Not having to make decisions or experience the pressures of work, all while watching grown men clobber each other, is quite relaxing. I could do it all day, and on some rare occasions I have. This rest is great in allowing time to relax physically and even mentally, but by itself it doesn't equip me to effectively handle that angry customer or the interoffice squabble waiting for me on Monday. Things like movies, televisions, sports, hobbies, or other entertainment are not bad, but if relaxation is all we focus on we are not strengthened for the challenges in life. Too often we seek diversion rather than confronting our real needs, and this diversion is what entertainment provides.[14] We have a high calling in a challenging environment and for that reason we need to be built up, not just diverted.

We should not think the Sabbath as a day for complete inactivity; it is a day to rest from work, so we can pursue God. Samuel Terrien said, "The seventh day did not call for a withdrawal of activity but for a renewal of vitality."[15] This renewal of vitality comes from activity that seeks God by keeping the day holy (Ex 20:8). The fact that we should have holy activities on this

---

[14] Blaise Pascal, *Pensees,* Order, VIII 139, p43. Pascal speaks of the place of diversion today.

[15] Samuel Terrien, *The Elusive Presence* (San Francisco: Harper & Row Publishers, 1978), 393.

day is the reason the Westminster Confession forbids "profaning the day by idleness" (WLC 119). If we spend the whole day only seeking relaxation, idleness, and diversion we fail to rightly observe it.

The main way to make this day holy is by looking to the Lord and dedicating it to him. On the Sabbath we pursue God, and it is in pursuit of him we receive edification. Historically the Sabbath has been interpreted as a day of being spiritually profitable. As J.I. Packer said, "We do not keep the Sabbath holy by lounging around doing nothing. We are to rest from the business of our earthly calling in order to pursue the business of our heavenly calling. If we do not spend the day doing the later, we fail to keep it holy."[16] Two main ways we keep this day holy are by participating in church and worship.

Attending a healthy church is a main way to sanctify the Sabbath and experience edifying rest. It is through church that we fellowship with other believers, hear the word of God preached, give and receive encouragement, and serve others. Church is a main way to gain direction, encouragement, and resolve to serve God in the world. It is so essential that Jesus himself made attending such services a habit (Luke 4:16).

An important part of attending church is hearing the word of God. The Heidleberg Catechism (HC 103) says that to make the day holy one should "diligently frequent the church of God." The benefits of attending church are numerous and hearing the right teaching of God's word is vital. The right teaching of God's word can have a profound effect on our lives. Psalm 19:7 says, "The law of the Lord is perfect, reviving the soul." When heard and received with faith the word of God brings vigor to our hearts, souls, and minds.

God's word is often described as a light, and it is the light of his word that helps us find our way through life. Had it not been for the faithful preaching of the word I would still be in darkness and confusion about many of the difficulties (and blessings) at the office (and home). God's word is a light that shines on our path to show us the right way to walk. I have gained much wisdom through the preached word that helped me navigate difficult

---

[16] Packer, 95.

situations, and moreover I am convinced that for every time the preached word directed me through a present difficulty it prevented a thousand difficulties by setting me on the right path from the very beginning.

I have no doubt that many fail in business because they have first failed with God. They have grown frustrated in work, because they don't understand the place of difficulties; they make bad decisions, because they do not know and obey God's word; they lose customers, because they do not know how to care for others. Our society is one familiar with God, but ignorant of his life changing truth. It is this life changing truth encountered through healthy churches on the day of rest that equips and builds people up for life.

In addition to attending church, we should also be edified through the act of worship. While it is easily argued that worship should be seen as part of church service, I single it out to draw attention to its special relation to the Sabbath. We appropriately make the day holy by spending time in worship of our great God and reflecting on the great hope we have in him. It can rightly be said, "Worship is the priority of the Lord's day."[17]

We worship to celebrate and declare God's steadfast love and faithfulness. As we reflect on his faithfulness, it leads to worshiping him. Our worship of him is not primarily about his involvement in our work, but his faithfulness to his plan of redemptive history. Our worship of God centers on his provision of a savior to save sinners and redeem the world from the effects of sin.

Celebrating what God has done by providing a savior leads to celebrating what we anticipate him doing at the end of history. In creation, God's six days of work culminate in the Sabbath. This is the only day of creation that does not conclude with the phrase "and there was morning and there was evening," and many take this to mean the Sabbath is the climax of creation that anticipates an eternal rest with God. [18] This never-ending rest is what Hebrews

---

[17] A.T. Lincoln, "From Sabbath to Lord's Day: A Biblical and Theological Perspective," in D.A. Carson, editor, *From Sabbath to Lord's Day* (Eugene: Wipf & Stock, 1982), 405.

[18] Terrien, 393.

4:9 refers to when is it says, "There remains then a Sabbath rest for the people of God."

The Sabbath points to the day when we will no longer labor and toil to bring God's kingdom on earth, because it will have arrived. At this time we will enter the very rest of God (Heb 4:10). This eternal rest is given when God's work of redemption is complete and his people are united with him in heaven. Our present rest should anticipate and rejoice in this glorious eternal rest that awaits us. As John Murray said,

> The Sabbath is… also the promise of a glorious prospect, the foretaste of the Sabbath rest that remains for the people of God. It is the prospect of the grand finale to the whole of history, the Sabbath rest that is the promised sequel to the sum total of the toils and labors of history.[19]

The Sabbath is a day to anticipate and celebrate the promised grand finale of history when God's redemptive acts are complete, and we dwell with him in glory. This glorious ending gives strength and hope to all we do.

Rest is not just a time to be idle, but it is a time to be built up and encouraged. We are to make it a holy time, a time dedicated to the Lord, and attending a healthy church and worshiping God are crucial to hallowing the day. Doing so observes God's pattern for rest and builds us up for the relentless trials that now come our way.

9.4 Turning to the Lord of Rest

Josh and his brothers planned a week-long guys-only trip to a beautiful but undeveloped island off the coast of Maryland. For a group of guys who love camping and the outdoors it was perfect. They got to see wild horses, fish on un-fished waters, and enjoy the quietude of having no one else around. It was perfect, until night came. That is when the mosquitoes on this hot swamp infested

---

[19] John Murray, *Collected Writings of John Murray,* vol 4 (Carlisle: Banner of Truth Trust, 1991), 216.

island came out in droves. This wouldn't normally be a problem had they not forgotten bug spray—a key element for any camping trip to such an island. This key element would be the down fall of their trip. The next day they were swollen from hundreds of bites and exhausted from no sleep. They left out a key component of their vacation, and as a result they got no rest.

Many of us also attempt to find rest but forget the key element. There is no greater lesson to the Sabbath than when Jesus said he is "The Lord of the Sabbath" (Mark 2:28, Matt 12:8). With this profound statement he teaches that true rest is not found in a day or time, but in him. As the Lord of rest, we ultimately look to Jesus for the restoration we need. He is the one who stands over rest, and he is the one who gives it. Without him we will never find rest.

The famous words of Psalm 23 colorfully show it is God who restores. It says, "The Lord is my shepherd I shall not be in want. He makes me lie down in green pastures, he leads me beside quiet waters, he restores my soul" (v1-3). In the midst of green pastures and quiet waters it is the Lord alone who gives rest and restores the soul.

Having our souls restored can seem a bit vague, but in Psalm 23 the word soul (nephesh) most likely refers to the passions, desires, or the drives of a person. It refers to God "bringing back the vigor of life."[20] Who would argue that in the midst of challenges we get worn down by burdens? We grow weary and faint. When bad news comes we struggle to get out of bed. In such times we lack vigor and vitality, and we need our drives and passions restored. We will never find this restoration by looking to hobbies and vacations alone. It is God who restores our souls, and we must ultimately turn to him. We will only find rest by heeding Jesus words, "Come to me, all you who are weary and burdened, and I will give you rest" (Matt 11:28).

Rest or relaxation without Jesus will never bring true rest. There can be some refreshment found in things like a nice drink (Psalm 104:15), good news (Prov 15:30), a big paycheck (Psalm 4:7), or a nice vacation, but these are not what we ultimately need.

---

[20] Hans Joachin Kraus, *Psalms*, vol 1, translated by Hilton C. Oswald (Mineaolis: Fortress Press, 1993), 307.

These cannot restore our inner being. Even reflecting on life, attending church, and worshipping is done in vain if it is not centered on drawing near to Jesus.

The joy and rest that come from Jesus is greater than anything else we can find, and rest that comes apart from him is but a shadow of the true. We receive his rest by faith (Heb 4:3). It is by believing our sin has been atoned for through Christ's death, and that we now have peace with God (Rom 5:1). Forgiveness of sins brings a peace that flows into every part of our life. Knowing we have peace with God gives us faith we can trust him to lead us in every situation. Our hearts are at rest because we are forgiven and because we have a good Lord who is with us and leading us.

If we are separated from God there is no true rest, because we are still in our sins and no matter what we receive it does not meet our greatest need, which is forgiveness of sins and life with God. Rest without rest in God is like a man with a terminal disease receiving a back massage. The massage may feel great, but it does not remove his condition, and because his underlying condition remains it is impossible to truly be comforted by the massage.

Until we experience resting in Christ, we will never experience rest in anything else. It is rest and peace with God that our hearts yearn for. It is as Augustine said, "You have made us for yourself and restless is our heart until it comes to rest in you."[21] Jesus is the one who gives us rest even in the busiest and most tumultuous times of our lives and vocations. If we have just returned from that killer vacation and find ourselves as restless as ever, it may be because we have been seeking rest without the key component—Jesus.

9.5 What it Takes to Rest

Knowing Jesus brings an anticipation of encountering soul-restoring rest in our time off. But despite the great benefits of rest and the confidence of meeting God, taking time off to look to him never comes easily, and for this reason we end with a couple

---

[21] Augustine, *Confessions,* trans Henry Chadwick (Oxford: Oxford University Press, 1998), 3.

practical tips on resting. Finding consistent and effective time off requires both discipline and trust in God.

Resting requires diligent work. If we are going to take time off from work we must make sure our work is done. If one is slack in his work he will never be able to get away. Taking time off begins with working effectively when we should be working. Taking one day a week off demands we work more effectively and strategically on the other days (and I would argue taking a day off is the beginning of working effectively and strategically). If we do not work when we are supposed to, we will never rest when we are supposed to.

If we want to spend time in the morning turning to the Lord of rest and having our soul revived through the word of God each day, it requires discipline the night before. Honoring the Sabbath requires working with discipline the other six days. A lack of discipline leads to working without rest and resting without ever working. We are unable to do one because of too much of the other. It is a vicious cycle where lack of discipline leads to lack of rest or too much rest leads to not enough work. The days become a smudge of colors, all running together to make one long indistinguishable blur of life. It is a work of drudgery having neither effective work nor effective rest.

In addition to working diligently, resting also requires trust in God. Only God gets his to-do list done, and we need to be able to rest even when things are left undone. We rest from our work, because our hope is in God, not our labors. A person who is inclined to work seven days a week should examine who their trust is in.[22]

In a way, resting is a test case for a much broader question—do we trust God? There is always more that can be done. Nothing is ever perfect, and even if it were it would not stay that way. Work will always need to be done. Busybodies will always find something to do. The issue is not having your work so well performed that it justifies resting, but rather that you trust God enough to rest when things are undone.

---

[22] Waltke, *An Old Testament Theology*, 424. This sentence is slightly adapted from Waltke.

Jesus came to the house of two sisters named Mary and Martha (Luke 10:38-42). Mary sat content at the feet of Jesus listening to his every word, while Martha busied herself about the house, and even complained that Mary didn't help with the preparations. When Martha asked Jesus about this, Jesus told her that Mary had chosen what was best. It may be unthinkable that Jesus would come to someone's house, and they would not listen to him, but Jesus offers rest to us every day, and we often do not heed his voice because we, like Martha, are too busy.

Like Mary we must put our duties aside and glean from the Lord of rest. More people need to be like Mary, who could sit content just being with her Lord. Our greatest threat of bondage to overwork is usually not oppressive bosses, but our own unsatisfied hearts. Our failures, feeble undertakings, and unfinished work need not bring us into bondage.[23] Trust in God frees us from such bondage.

9.6 Reflections on Retirement

In rest our trust in God is constantly tested, and it will also be tested as we draw closer to our day of final rest. As we grow ever closer to the day we stand before God, we very well may enter a time of diminished effectiveness that leads to stepping away from full time work. For many it will take great faith to step away from grueling work schedules and no longer be identified with their career. John Cotton points out the confidence with which a Christian should enter this time saying, "Another man when his calling comes to be removed from him, he is much ashamed and much afraid; but if a Christian man is to forego his calling, he lays it down with comfort and boldness in the sight of God."[24] When this time comes it will take humility and trust in God to step back and let another take our place.

If or when it is necessary to retire we should do so with boldness, because our trust is in God, but this does not mean we

---

[23] Lincoln, 405.

[24] John Cotton, *The Way of Life or God's Way and Course* (London, 1641; reprinted by Kessinger Publishing), 446.

cease to exercise dominion. As long as a person is alive, he should be exploring ways to influence the world. Even in old age one should seek to further God's purposes through dominion. Work may be lessened in intensity, duration, and complexity, but it should never be forsaken. While some things may change there should still be a pattern of six days of work and one day of rest.

Far too many people today retire too early in life and forfeit one of the greatest means of influencing the world for the kingdom of God. But it would be an exaggerated view of work to think that for most people there will not come a time when they simply are not as effective in their jobs as is required. Time for retirement should be marked more by diminishing effectiveness rather than a desire not to work. It is poor stewardship to have a gift and never use it, and it's just as bad to quit using a gift when it still works fine. Too many people retire because the world is their treasure, and they do not really care about influencing it for the glory of God.

9.7 Conclusion

Rest is good and working effectively for the glory of God requires resting effectively for the glory of God. Everyone should have consistent patterns of daily, weekly, and special rest to provide for their physical and spiritual needs. True rest, that is rest that restores souls, comes only through Jesus Christ, and it is for that reason we seek him chiefly in our rest. Jesus is the one who gives rest to the weary and restores souls, and very often the way he does it is through proper observance of the gift of rest. Proper observance of rest includes reflecting, relaxing, and being edified through the word of God and worship of God.

We must be diligent in our work and put our trust in God in order to rest. People often fail to rest, because they fail to work effectively, or because they fail to trust God and always find one more thing to do. Ultimately people who fail to rest fail to make God their all in all. Just as we work to the glory of God we also rest to the glory of God. It is only when God becomes our all in all that we find true rest, and it is not until resting completely in him that we are able to work for true glory and do work that really matters.

Chapter 9 Discussion Questions

1. What are your greatest struggles in glorifying God through rest?

2. What type of rest do you most often neglect?

3. What does your lack of rest reveal about your priorities, trust, and work ethic?

4. What goals and benefits of rest are most helpful for you to hear about and why?

Bibliography

Alexander, T.D., *From Paradise to Promise Land: An Introduction to the Pentateuch.* Carlisle: Paternoster Press, 2002.

Alexander, T. Desmond and Brian S. Rosner, D.A. Carson and Graeme Goldsworthy editors. *New Dictionary of Biblical Theology.* Downers Grove: InterVarsity Press, 2000.

Anderson, Fil, Robert A. Fryling, Craig M. Glass and Stephen W. Smith. *Work.* Downers Grove: Inter-Varsity Press, 2006.

Atkinson, David. *The Message of Genesis 1-11.* The Bible Speaks Today. Downers Grove: Inter-Varsity Press, 1990.

Augustine. *Confessions.* Trans Henry Chadwick. Oxford: Oxford University Press, 1998.

a` Kempis, Thomas. *Imitation of Christ.* Nashville: Thomas Nelson Publishers, 1999.

Badcock, Gary D. *The Way of Life.* Grand Rapids: Eerdmans, 1998.

Bavinck, Herman. *Essays on Religion, Science, and Society.* Edited by John Bolt and translated by Harry Boonstra and Gerrit Sheeres. Grand Rapids: Baker Academic, 2008.

_____. *Reformed Dogmatics.* Edited by John Bolt. Translated by John Friend. 4 vols. Grand Rapids: Baker Academic, 2006.

Beal, G. K. *The Temple and the Church's Mission: A Biblical Theology of the Dwelling Place of God.*

_____. New Studies in Biblical Theology 17. Downers Grove: Intervarsity Press, 2004. *We Become What we Worship.* Downers Grove: Inter-Varsity Press, 2008.

Beek, Joel R., editor. *Living for God's Glory: An Introduction to Calvinism.* Reformation Trust Publishing: Orlando, 2008

Berkhoff, Louis. *Systematic Theology.* Grand Rapids: Eerdmans, 1996.

Bloesch, Donald G. *The Church.* Downers Grove: InterVarsity Press, 2002.

Bloomberg, Craig. *The New American Commentary.* Edited by David Dockery. Vol. 22. Nashville, TN: Broadman Press, 1992.

Bock, Darrell L. *Luke: 1:1-19:50.* Baker Exegetical Commentary. Grand Rapids: Baker Books, 1994.

Brakel, Wilhelmus. The Chrsitians Reasonable Service. Vol 3,4. Translated by Bartel Elshout. Edited by Joel Beeke. Grand Rapids: Reformation Heritage Books, 2007.

Bridges, Jerry. "Does Divine Sovereignty Make a Difference in Every Day Life," in Bruce Ware and Thomas R. Shreiner, editors. *Still Sovereign.* Grand Rapids: Baker Books, 2003.

Bruce, F.F. *Apostle of the Heart Set Free.* Grand Rapids: William B. Eerdmans Publishing, 1977.

_____. *Epistle to the Galatians.* Grand Rapids: William B. Eerdmans Publishing Company, 1982.

Bunyan, John. *The Pilgrims Progress.* New York: Penguin, 1987.

Calvin, John. *Commentaries on Genesis.* trans John King. Grand Rapids: Baker Books, 2005.

_____. *Institutes.* 2 Vols. Edited by John T. McNeil and translated by Ford Lewis Battles Louisville: Westminster John Knox Press, 1960.

Carson, D.A.,editor. *From Sabbath to Lords's Day:A Biblical, Historical, and Theological Investigation.* Eugene: Wipf and Stock Publishers, 1982.

Carson, D.A. *How Long O Lord?* Grand Rapids: Inter-Varsity Press, 1990.

Charnock, Stephen. *The Existence and Attributes of God.* Minneapolis: Klock&Klock Christian Publishers, 1969.

Clowney, Edmund. *The Church.* Downers Grove: InterVarsity Press, 1995.

Collins, Jim. *Good to Great.* New York: Harper Collins, 2001.

Cotton, John. *The Way of Life or God's Way and Course.* London, 1641; reprinted by Kessinger Publishing.

Dabney, R.L. *The Practical Philosophy.* Harrisonburg: Sprinkle, 1984.

Davies, W.D. and D.C. Allison. *Matthew 1-7.* International Critical Commentary. Vol. I. London: T&T Clark International, 1988.

Dumbrell, William. *Covenant and Creation.* Mt. Radford: Paternoster, 1984.

Ebbing, Darrell D. *General Chemistry.* Boston: Houghton Mifflin Company, 1996.

Edwards, Jonathan. *The Religious Affections.* Edinburgh: Banner of Truth Trust, 1997.

186

_____. *The Works of Jonathan Edwards*. 2 vols. Carlisle: Banner of Truth Trust, 1998.

Eichrodt, Walther. Theology of the Old Testament. 2 Vols. Translated by J.A. Baker. Philadelphia: Westminster Press, 1976.

Estes, Daniel. *Handbook on the Wisdom Books and Psalms.* Grand Rapids: Baker Academic, 2005.

Fee, Gordon. *The Disease of the Health and Wealth Gospels.* Costa Mesa, CA: The Word For Today, 1979.

Ferguson, Sinclair. *The Christian Life.* Carlisle: Banner of Truth Trust, 1981.

Frame, John. *Doctrine of God.* Phillipsburg: P&R Publishing, 2002.

_____. *Doctrine of the Christian Life.* Phillipsburg: P&R Publishing, 2008.

France, R.T. *The Gospel of Matthew.* Grand Rapids: Eerdmans, 2007.

_____ *Tyndale New Testament Commentaries: Matthew.* Grand Rapids: Eerdmans, 1985.

Goff, James R. Jr. "The Faith That Claims." *Christianity Today,* vol. 34, February 1990.

Grudem, Wayne. *Systematic Theology: An Introduction to Biblical Doctrine.* Grand Rapids: Zondervan, 1994.

Guiness, Os. *The Call: Finding and Fulfilling the Central Purpose of Your Life.* Nashville: Thomas Nelson, 2003.

Hamilton, Victor P. *The Book of Genesis.* Vol 1. New American Commentary 1A. Grand Rapids: William B. Eerdmans Publishing Company, 1990.

Hammond, Pete, and R. Paul Stevens, and Todd Svanoe. *The Marketplace Annotated Bibliography.* Downers Grove: InterVarsity Press, 2002.

Hansel, Tim. *When I Relax I Feel Guilty.* Elgen, IL: David C Cook, 1979.

Harris, Laird, Gleason Archer, and Bruce Waltkke. *Theological Wordbook of the Old Testament* . Chicago: Moody Press, 1980.

Heppe, Heinrich. *Reformed Dogmatics,* trans G.T. Thompson, Editor Ernst Bizer. Grand Rapids: Baker Book House.

Hodge, Charles. *Systematic Theology.* 3 Vols. Grand Rapids: Eerdmans, 1999.

Hoekema, Anthony. *Bible and the Future. Grand Rapids: William B. Eerdmans, 1979.*

Hoekema, Anthony. *Created in God's Image.* Grand Rapids: Eerdmans, 1994.

Jenni, Ernst and Claus Westermann. *Theological Lexicon of the Old Testament.* Peabody, MA: Hendrickson Publishers, 1997.

Jones, David. "The Bankruptcy of the Prosperity Gospel: An Exercise in Biblical Theological Ethics," n.p. (Cited 19 Nov 2009). Online: http://bible.org/article/bankruptcy-prosperity-gospel-exercise-biblical-and-theological-ethics.

Keller, Tim *Counterfeit Gods.* Dutton: New York, 2009.

Kidner, Derek. *Genesis.* Downers Grove: Inter-Varsity Press, 1967.

_____. *Proverbs: An Introduction and Com*mentary. Tyndale Old Testament Commentary. Downers Grove: Inter-Varsity press, 1964.

Kline, Meredith. *Kingdom Prologue.* Overland Park: Two Ages Press, 2000.

Kraus, Hans Joachin. *Psalms.* Vol 1. Translated by Hilton C. Oswald. Mineaolis: Fortress Press, 1993.

Kuiper, R.B. *The Glorius Body of Christ.* Carlisle: Banner of Truth Trust, 2001.

Kuyper, Abraham. *A Centinial Reader.* Edited by James D. Bratt Grand Rapids: William B. Eerdmans, 1998.

Lloyd-Jones, Martin. *Spiritual Depression: Its Causes and Cure.* Grand Rapids: Eerdmans Publishing Company.

Longman, Tremper. *Proverbs.* Grand Rapids: Baker, 2006

Luther, Martin. *The Works of Luther.* Edited by Jaroslav Pelikan and Helmut T. Lehmann. 55 Vols. Saint Louis: Concordia Publishing, 1963.

MacArthur, John. *Matthew 1-7.* The Testament Commentary Chicago, IL: Moody Press, 1985.

Matthews, Kenneth. *Genesis 1-11:26.* New American Commentary. Nashville: Broadman and Holman Publishers, 2002.

McGrath, Alister. *Reformation Thought: An Introduction.* Oxford: Blackwell Publishing, 1999.

Merrril, Eugene. *Kingdom of Priests.* Grand Rapids: Baker Books, 1987.

Miller, Darrow. *Lifework.* Seattle: YWAM, 2009.

Morgan, Edmund S, editor. *Puritan Political Ideas: 1558-1794.* Indianapolis: Hackett Publishing Company, 2003.

Morris, Leon. *The Gospel According to Matthew.* Grand Rapids: Eerdmans Publishing Company, 1992.

Murray, John. *Collected Writings of John Murray.* Vol 4. Carlisle: Banner of Truth Trust, 1991.

_____. *Principles of Conduct.* Grand Rapids: Eerdmans, 1957.

Nolland, John. *Word Biblical Commentary, Luke 1-9:20.* Edited by hubbard David. Nashville, TN: Thomas Nelson Pub, 1989.

Packer, J.I. "The Puritans and the Lord's Day" in J.I. Packer, editor, *Puritan Paperbacks.* Vol 1. Phillipsburg: P&R Publishing, 2000.

Pascal, Blaise. *Pensees.* Translated by A.J. Krailsheimer. London: Penguin Books, 1995.

Paul II, John. *Encyclical On Human Work: Laborem Exercens.* Boston: Daughters of St Paul, 1981.

Perkins, William. "William Perkings on Callings" in Morgan, Edmund S. *Puritan Political Ideas: 1558-1794."* Indianapolis: Hacket Publishing, 1965.

Peters, George. *A Biblical Theology of Missions.* Chicago: Moody Press, 1972.

Piper, John. *Amazing Grace in the Life of William Wilberforce.* Wheaton: Crossway, 2006.

Piper, John. *God is the Gospel.* Wheaton: Crossway Books, 2005.

Plato. *Republic.* Trans Robin Waterfield, Oxford: Oxford University Press, 1993.

Powlison, David. *Seeing With New Eyes.* Phillipsburg: P&R Publishing, 2003.

Preece, Gordon. "Work," in *The Complete Book of Everyday Christianity.* Downers Grove, IL: InterVarsity, 1997.

Osteen, Joel. *Your Best Life Now.* New York: Faith Words, 2004.

Owen, John. *The Works of John Owen,* Vol 2. Carlisle, PA: Banner of Truth Trust, 1997.

Reymond, Robert. A New Systematic Theology of the Christian Faith. Nashville: Nelson, 1998.

Richardson, Allan. *The Biblical Doctrine of Work.* London: SCM Press, 1952.

Ridderbos, Herman. *Paul: An Outline of His Theology*. Translated by John Richard De Witt. Grand Rapids: William B. Eerdmans Publishing Company, 1997.

Rousas, John Rushdoony. *Institutes of Biblical Law: Law and Society.* 2 Vols. Vallecito: Ross House Books, 1986.

Ryken, Leland. *Redeeming the Time*. Grand Rapids: Baker Books, 1995.

_____. *Worldly Saints: The Puritans as the Really Were.* Grand Rapids: Zondervan, 1990.

_____, James C. Wilhoit, Tremper Longman III, general editors. *Dictionary of Biblical Imagery.* Downers Grove: InterVarsity Press, 1998.

Ryken, Phillip. *Galatians.* Phillipsburg: P&R Publishing, 2005.

Ryle, J.C. *Matthew.* Wheaton: Crossway, 1993.

Sander, Oswald. *Spiritual Leadership.* Chicago: Moody Publishers, 1994.

Sayers, Dorothy. *Creed or Chaos.* New York: Harcourt, Brace and Company, 1949.

Stevens, R. Paul. *The Other Six Days.* Grand Rapids: William B. Eerdmans Publishing Company, 1999.

Tenney, Merrill C, editor. *The Zondervan Pictoral Encyclopedia of the Bible.* 3 vols. Grand Rapids: Zondervan, 1976.

Terrien, Samuel. *The Elusive Presence.* San Francisco: Harper & Row Publishers, 1978.

Tozer, A.W., *The Knowledge of the Holy.* San Francisco: Harper Collins, 1961.

Tripp, Paul David. *Instruments of Change.* Philipsburg: P&R Publishing, 2002.

Veith, Gene Edward. *God at Work: Your Christian Vocation in All of Life.* Wheaton: Crossway, 2002.

Volf, Miroslav. *Work in the Spirit: Toward a Theology of Work.* Eugene: Wipf and Stock Publishers, 2001.

Von Rad, Gerhard. *Old Testament Theology.* Translated by D.M.G. Stalker. Vol 1. New York; Harper Row, 1962.

_____. *Genesis.* Old Testament Library. Philadelphia:

Westminster Press, 1972.

Waltke, Bruce. *An Old Testament Theology: An Exegetical, Canonical, and Thematic Approach.* Grand Rapids: Zondervan, 2006.

_____. *Genesis.* Grand Rapids: Zondervan, 2001.

_____. *The Book of Proverbs.* 2 Vols. The New International Commentary on the Old Testament. Grand Rapids: William B. Eerdmans Publishing Company, 2005.

Warrfield, B.B. *Selected Shorter Writings.* Vol 1. Phillipsburg: P&R Publishing, 1970.

Wenham, Gordon. *Genesis.* Vol 1. Word Biblical Commentary 1. Nashville: Nelson, 1987.

Westermann, Claus. *Genesis 1-11.* Minneapolis: Fortress Press, 1994.

Wingren, Gustaf. *Luther on Vocation.* Translated by Carl C Rasmussen. Eugene, OR: Wipf & Stock, 2004.

Wolff, Hans Walter. *Anthropology of the Old Testament.* Miffintown, PA: Singler Press Edition, 1996

Wright, Christopher. *Mission of God.* Downers Grove: InterVarsity Press, 2006.

_____. *Old Testament Ethics and the People of God.* Downers Grove: Intervarsity Press, 2004.

Made in the USA
Middletown, DE
03 June 2015